YO-ACY-954

Vest Pocket
FRENCH

Formerly published as: FRENCH IN A NUTSHELL

By
JOSEPH SOUTHAM CHOQUETTE
Government Language Instructor and Consultant

PUBLISHED BY
INSTITUTE FOR LANGUAGE STUDY
Montclair, New Jersey 07042

DISTRIBUTED TO THE BOOK TRADE BY
BARNES & NOBLE BOOKS
A DIVISION OF HARPER & ROW, *PUBLISHERS*

Library of Congress Catalog Card Number: 58-8917
First paperbound edition published 1967 by Funk & Wagnalls,

Published by arrangement with Institute for Language Study

© COPYRIGHT 1958 BY INSTITUTE FOR LANGUAGE STUDY

All Rights Reserved

This material is fully protected under the terms of the
Universal Copyright Convention.   It is specifically
prohibited to reproduce this publication in any form
whatsoever, including sound recording, photocopying, or
by use of any other electronic reproducing, transmitting
or retrieval system.   Violators will be prosecuted to the
full extent provided by law.

Printed in the United States of America

9 8 7 6 5 4 3 2

TABLE OF CONTENTS

3

GETTING THE MOST OUT OF YOUR COURSE

THE WORLD is growing smaller every day. Far-sighted people who recognize the value of speaking a second language will reap the benefits of greater business success, more traveling enjoyment, easier study and finer social relationships.

VEST POCKET FRENCH will unlock for you the treasure house of learning a language the easy way, with a fresh, new approach—without monotonous drills. Before you know it, you'll be speaking your new language easily and without embarrassment. You will be able to converse with fascinating people from other lands and read books and magazines from their country in the original language.

Much research and painstaking study has gone into the "Vest Pocket" method of learning a new language as easily as possible. This Course is the result of that research, and for the reader's convenience it is divided into several basic, closely related sections.

The KEY TO PRONUNCIATION explains the sounds of the language. Each sentence is accompanied by the phonetic spelling to help you learn the pronunciation. This method has been tested extensively and found to be the best to enable the student to associate sounds with written forms.

The BASIC SENTENCE PATTERNS are the unique new approach to sentence construction. Here you will find sentence patterns needed in general conversation. On these basic patterns you can build sentences to suit your own particular needs.

The EVERYDAY CONVERSATIONS form the main section of this book. Here you will find a large number of situations useful for general language learning and traveling purposes. You will learn hundreds upon hundreds of conversational sentences you may need to make yourself understood. Even more important, the material is organized to provide you with a wide basis for varying the vocabulary and sentences as much as your interest and ingenuity might desire.

The OUTLINE OF GRAMMAR provides a rapid understanding of the grammatical structure of your new language. The "Basic Sentence Patterns" are closely correlated with this section to give you a quick knowledge of the language.

The two-way DICTIONARY of over 6500 entries includes all the words used in the Everyday Conversations and contains another 3000 frequently used words and expressions. It thus forms a compact and invaluable tool for the student.

Here are the tools. Use them systematically, and before you know it you will have a "feeling" for the new language. The transcriptions furnish authentic reproduction of the language to train your ear and tongue to the foreign sounds; thus you can SEE the phrase, SAY the phrase, HEAR the phrase, and LEARN the phrase.

Remember that repetition and practice are the foundation stones of language learning. Repeat and practice what you have learned as often as you can. You will be amazed (and your friends will, too) how quickly you have acquired a really practical knowledge of French.

THE EDITORS

KEY TO FRENCH PRONUNCIATION

First let us remind you of a few basic facts:

1) French is not an accentuated language like English, therefore each phrase should be spoken *evenly*, the last syllable and last word of the phrase being given a little stronger inflection.

2) Contrary to English, the vowels are the important elements each of them should be pronounced very distinctly and never be slurred as they sometimes are in English.

VOWELS

FRENCH SPELLING	PHONETIC SYMBOL	DESCRIPTION	EXAMPLES
a, â	ah	As *a* in *father*.	*gras* (grah) fat; *pâte* (paht) dough
a	ah	Almost as *a* in *hat*.	*balle* (bahl) ball; *classe* (klahs) class
e	uh	Somewhat like the unstressed *e* in *the*.	*petite* (puh-teet) small; *retour* (ruh-toor) retur_
é	ay	As *a* in *maybe*.	*beauté* (boh-tay) beauty; *étoile* (ay-twahl) star
è, ê	eh	As *e* of *led*.	*père* (pehr) father; *tête* (teht) head

i, î	ee	As *i* in *machine*.	*pipe* (peep) pipe; *île* (eel) island
o, ô	oh	As *o* in *so*.	*chose* (shohz) thing; *diplôme* (dee-plohm) diploma
o	oh	As *o* in *loss*.	*col* (kohl) collar; *poche* (pohsh) pocket
u, û	ew	Round the lips as if to say *oo*, but pronounce *ee*.	*utile* (ew-teel) useful; *brûler* (brew-lay) burn

COMBINATIONS OF VOWELS

FRENCH SPELLING	PHONETIC SYMBOL	DESCRIPTION	EXAMPLES
ai	ay	*é;* as *a* in maybe.	*mai* (may) May; *prendrai* (prahng-dray) I shall take
ei	eh	*è;* as *e* in *led*.	*neige* (nehzh) snow; *beige* (behzh) beige
au, eau	oh	*o;* as *o* in *so*.	*auto* (oh-toh) auto; *bateau* (bah-toh) boat
eu, oeu	uh	Round the lips as if to say *oo*, but pronounce *ay*.	*feu* (fuh) fire; *coeur* (kuhr) heart
oi	wah	as *wa* in *watch*.	*loi* (lwah) law; *boîte* (bwaht) box
ou	oo	as *oo* in *food*.	*bijou* (bee-zhoo) jewel; *mouche* (moosh) fly
ui	wee	as *wee* in *week*.	*cuisine* (kwee-zeen) cuisine; *bruit* (brweet) noise

NASAL VOWEL SOUNDS

FRENCH SPELLING	PHONETIC SYMBOL	DESCRIPTION	EXAMPLES
am, an em, en	ahng	As *a* in *father*, but nasalized.	*ample* (ahng-pluh) ample; *manteau* (mahng-toh) coat; *emploi* (ahng-plwah) job; *entier* (ahng-tyay) entire

[important;

im, in	**ang**	Almost as *a* in *man,*	*important* (ang-pohr-tahng)
aim, ain		but nasalized.	*inquiet* (ang-kyay) worried;
ein			*faim* (fang) hunger;
			main (mang) hand;
			plein (plang) full
om, on	**ohng**	As *o* in *north,* but nasalized.	*ombre* (ohng-bruh) shade;
			bonbon (bohng-bohng) candy
um, un	**uhng**	As *u* in *fur,* but nasalized.	*parfum* (pahr-fuhng) perfume
			chacun (shah-kuhng) each
ien	**yang**		*chien* (shyang) dog;
			rien (ryang) nothing
oin	**wang**		*besoin* (buh-zwang) need;
			coin (kwang) corner
uin	**ewang**		*juin* (zhewang) June

A vowel is nasalized when it is followed by an *m* or *n* at the end of a word, or in any other position of the word when *m* or *n* is followed by a consonant other than *m* or *n*. In these cases, *m* and *n* indicate the nasalization of the preceding vowel but are not pronouced.

SPECIAL SOUNDS

FRENCH SPELLING	PHONETIC SYMBOL	DESCRIPTION	EXAMPLES
r	**r**	Place front of tongue behind lower teeth and raise back of tongue toward soft palate—almost a soft gargle.	*roi* (rwah) king; *rapide* (rah-peed) rapid; *porte* (pohr-t) door; *artiste* (ahr-teest) artist
s	**s**	Generally like the English *s* but like the English *z* between two vowels.	*salle* (sahl) room; *moustache* (moo-stahsh) moustache; *maison* (meh-zohng) house; *raser* (rah-zay) shave
ch	**sh**	Never as *ch* in *chair,* always as *sh* in *wish.*	*chaise* (shehz) chair; *tache* (tahsh) stain
gn	**ny**	as *ni* in *onion.*	*montagne* (mohng-tahny) mountain; *cogner* (coh-nyay) knock

ill	eey	as *y* in *yes*.	*fille* (feey) girl; *famille* (fah-meey) family
ail, aille	ahy	as *uy* in *buy*, lingering on the *y* sound.	*travail* (trah-vahy) work; *paille* (pahy) straw
eil, eille	ehy	as *a* of *may*, lingering on the *y* sound.	*réveil* (ray-vehy) alarm clock; *bouteille* (boo-tehy) bottle
tion, tieu	syohng syuh	in such combinations, the *t* is pronounced like the English *s*.	*nation* (nah-syohng) nation; *ambitieux* (ahng-bee-syuh) ambitious;
tien	see-ahng		*patient* (pah-see-ahng) patient;
tie	see		*diplomatie* (dee-ploh-mah-see) diplomacy.

CONSONANTS

b, d, f, k, l, m, n, p, q, t, v, and **z** have almost the same sounds as they have in English.

c   As *k* in *kick*, at the end of a word, before a consonant or before *a, o, u: lac* (lahk) lake; *crème* (krehm) cream; *carte* (kahrt) card.

As *s* in *see* before *e, i, y,* or when written with a cedilla (ç) before *a, o, u:* ciel (syehl) heaven; français (frahng-seh) French.

g   As *g* in *go*, before a consonant or *a, o, u:* gloire (glwahr) glory; *gateau* (gah-toh) cake.

As *s* in *pleasure*, before *e, i, y:* gens (zhahn) people.

h   Never pronounced.

j   As *s* in *pleasure:* jardin (zhahr-dang) garden.

x   As *gz* between two vowels; *examen* (ehg-zah-mang) examination.

As *ks* when followed by a consonant: *excuse* (ehks-kewz) excuse.

Occasionally as *ss: dix* (dees) ten.

ph is pronounced like *f,* and **th** like *t.*
c, f, l, r are generally pronounced at the end of a word, the other consonants are not.

ELISION AND LIAISON

In order to keep the musical quality of their language, the French avoid unpleasant sounds or disrupted speech and link their words together in the following manner:

1) **Elision:** In order not to pronounce two vowels one after the other, the last vowel of a word disappears when the following word also begins with a vowel. An apostrophe (') takes the place of the missing vowel: *l'école (la école), il m'attend (me attend).*

2) **Liaison** The last consonant of a word is sometimes pronounced together with the initial vowel of the next one especially if these two words are in close connection (article and noun; subject and verb.)

In a "liaison" some consonants change their sounds:

s and *x* become *z*	*les enfants (le zenfants)* the children; *deux élèves (deu-zélèves)* two students.
d becomes *t*	*Entend-il? (enten-til)* Does he understand?
f often becomes *v*	*neuf-ans (neu-vans)* nine years.

WRITTEN ACCENTS

The accents you see on French words do not indicate a stressed syllable, but they either change the pronunciation of a vowel or differentiate two words spelled alike.

1) **Accent aigu** (´)—Used only on the letter *e,* it gives it the sound of an English accented *a* in words like April, but still shorter.

2) **Accent grave** (`)—When placed over the letter *e,* it gives it the open sound of the English *e* in words like *led.* It is also used on the letter *a* to distinguish between *a* (has) and *à* (at, to) and *la* (the *f.*) and *là* (there).

3) **Accent circonflexe** (^)—It gives the letter *e* the same sound as the *è.* On *a* or *o,* it indicates that the vowel is long. On *i* or *u,* it does not change the pronunciation of the vowel but indicates that these vowels were formerly followed by an *s* (*île*—island, the *s* has been retained in the English word.)

BASIC SENTENCE PATTERNS

In each language there are a few basic types of sentences which are used more often than others in everyday speech.

On the basis of such sentences, it is possible to form many others by substituting one or two of the words of each of these basic sentences. The phrases and sentences selected to illustrate the basic patterns are short, easy to memorize and useful. Learning them before you tackle the main section with the phrases covering everyday needs and travel situations, you will acquire an idea of the structure of the language. You will also learn indirectly through these basic types of sentences some of the most important grammatical categories and their function in the construction of the sentences the natural way—the way they are encountered in actual usage.

Cross references have been supplied to establish a correlation between the basic sentence patterns and the Grammar section in this book. This will help you to relate the grammatical knowledge you'll acquire passively going through the sentences to the systematic presentation of the basic facts of grammar. For example, when you encounter the phrase "See 4.9" in the first group of sentences, it means that by turning to chapter 4, subdivision 9 in the Grammar section you will find a description of the interrogative pronouns and their uses.

SIMPLE QUESTIONS AND ANSWERS
(See 4.9; 4.1; 2.1; 3.2; 8.7)

Qui est-il?	**C'est mon père (mon oncle, mon grand-père).**
kee-eh-teel'?	*seh mohng pehr' (mohn ohng-kl, mohng grahng-pehr').*
Who is he?	He is my father (uncle, grandfather).

Qui est-elle?	**C'est ma mère (ma tante, ma grand-mère).**
kee-eh-tehl'?	*seh mah mehr (mah tahng'-t, mah grahng-mehr').*
Who is she?	She is my mother (aunt, grandmother).

11

Qui est ce petit garçon?
*kee eh suh puh-tee
  gar-sohng'?*
Who is that boy?

C'est mon frère (mon cousin, mon neveu).
*seh mohng frehr'
(mohng koo-zang', mohng nuh-vuh').*
He is my brother (cousin, nephew).

Qui est l'autre jeune homme?
kee eh lohtr zhuhn ohm?
Who is the other boy?

C'est mon frère aîné.
seh mohng frehr' eh-nay'.
That's my older brother.

Qui est cette jeune fille?
kee eh seht zhuhn feey'?
Who is that girl?

C'est ma soeur cadette (cousine, nièce).
seh mah-suhr' kah-deht' (koo-zeen', nyehs').
She is my younger sister (cousin, niece).

Qui sont-ils (elles)?
kee-sohng-teel' (sohng-tehl')?
Who are they?

Ce sont mes grands-parents.
suh sohng meh grahng-pah-rahng'.
They are my grandparents.

Cette grande jeune fille est mon amie. (See 3.3)
seht grahngd zhun feey' eh mohn ah-mee'.
That tall girl is my girl friend.

Est-ce vrai?
eh-suh vreh'?
Is that so?

Où est mon chapeau? (See 5.3)
oo' eh mohng-shah-poh'?
Where is my hat?

Le voici.
luh vwah-see'.
Here it is.

Où est votre serviette?
oo' eh vohtr ser-vyet'?
Where is your briefcase?

Elle est là-bas.
ehl-eh lah-bah'.
It's over there.

Où est son sac à main?
oo' eh sohng sahk-ah-mang'?
Where's her handbag?

Il est ici.
eel eh tee-see'.
It's here.

Où sont les lavabos?
oo sohng leh lah-vah-boh'?
Where's the washroom?

C'est à droite (à gauche).
seh tah drwaht' (tah gohsh').
It's on the right (on the left).

Où est la chambre de Jean?
oo' eh lah shahng'-br duh zhahng?
Where is John's room?

En face, dans le couloir.
ahng fahs, dahng luh koo-lwahr'.
Across the corridor.

Où est la chambre de Louise?
oo' eh lah shahng'-br duh loo-weez'?
Where is Louise's room?

C'est un étage plus haut.
seh tuhng' ay-tahzh' plew oh'.
It's one flight up.

(See also 3.3; 4.7)

Qui a mes cahiers? Paul les a.
kee' ah meh kah-yay'? pohl leh zah'.
Who has my notebooks? Paul has them.

Avec qui parliez vous? Avec mon ami Pierre.
ah-vehk kee' pahr-lyay' voo? ahvehk monh nah-mee' pyehr.
With whom were you talking? With my friend Peter.

Qui sont ces messieurs? Ce sont des amis de mon fils.
kee' sohng seh meh-syuh'? suh sohng' deh zah-mee' duh mohng fees'.
Who are those men? They are my son's friends.

Qui sont ces jeunes filles? Ce sont les camarades d'école de ma fille.
kee' sohng seh zhuhn feey? suh sohng' leh kah-mah-rahd' day-kohl' duh mah feey'.
Who are those girls? They are my daughter's schoolmates.

Qu'est-ce qu'elle a dit? Elle a dit qu'elle ne pouvait pas venir.
kehs kehl ah dee'? ehl ah dee' kehl n-poo-veh pah' v-neer.
What did she say? She said she couldn't come.

Qu'est-ce que l'amour? C'est une chose merveilleuse.
kehs' kuh lah-moor? seh tewn shohz mehr-veh-yuhz'.
What is love? It's a wonderful thing.

Lequel de ces livres aimez-vous le mieux? Celui-ci.
luh-kehl' duh seh leevr' eh-may-voo' luh myuh? suh-lwee-see'.
Which one of these books do you like best? This one.

Quel est votre métier? Je suis vendeur.
kehl' eh vohtr may-tyay'? zhuh swee vahng-duhr'.
What is your occupation? I am a salesman.

SENTENCES WITH *HIM, HER* AND *IT*
(*Personal Object Pronouns*, See 4.1-2; 8.3-6)

Jean le lui a donné.
zhahng luh lwee ah doh-nay'.
John gave it to him.

Je le lui ai donné.
zhuh luh lwee ay doh-nay'.
I gave it to her.

Il me l'a donné.
eel muh lah doh-nay'.
He gave it to me.

Elle nous l'a envoyé.
ehl noo-lah ahng-vwah-yay'.
She sent it to us.

Nous vous l'avons donné.
noo voo lah-vohng doh-nay'.
We gave it to you.

Vous ne le leur avez pas donné.
voo nuh luh luhr ah-vay pah' doh-nay'.
You did not give it to them.

Donnez-le-moi.
doh-nay' luh-mwah'.
Give it to me.

Ne le lui donnez pas.
nuh luh lwee doh-nay pah'.
Don't give it to him.

Envoyez-le-lui.
ahng-vwah-yay-luh-lwee.
Send it to her.

Envoyez-le-nous par la poste.
ahng-vwah-yay-luh-noo' pahr lah pohst'.
Mail it to us.

Ne le leur envoyez pas par la poste.
nuh luh luhr ahng-vwah-yay pah pahr lah pohst.
Don't mail it to them.

SENTENCES ON THE USE OF *THE, AN* AND *A* (*The Articles,* See 1.1-5)

Le château est sur la montagne.
luh shah-toh eh sewr lah mohng-tahn'y'.
The castle is on the mountain.

L'appartement est à louer.
lah-pahr-tuh-mahng' eh tah loo-ay'.
The apartment is for rent.

Les Etats-Unis sont un grand pays.
leh-zay-tah-zewnee sohng tuhng grahng peh-ee'.
The United States is a big country.

Voici une paire de chaussons neufs.
vwah-see' ewn pehr duh shoh-sohng nuhf'.
Here is a pair of new slippers.

Je cherche le rayon des meubles.
zhuh shehrsh' luh reh-yohng' day muhbl'.
I am looking for the furniture department.

Il vend du papier à lettres et de la bijouterie.
eel vahng dew pah-pyehr ah laytr' ay duh lah bee-zhoo-tree'.
He sells stationery and jewelry.

Irez-vous aux sports d'hiver?
ee-ray-voo' oh spohr dee-vehr'?
Will you attend the winter sports?

Nous rentrons à la maison tout de suite.
noo rahng-trohng ah lah meh-zohng too-duh-sweet'.
We are going home right away.

Elle a les cheveux blonds et les yeux bleus.
el ah leh shuh-vuh blohng' ay leh zhyuh bluh'.
She has blonde hair and blue eyes.

Ils habitent Avenue des Amériques.
eel zah-beet' ah-vuh-new deh zah-may-reek'.
They live on the Avenue of the Americas.

Quel dommage!	**Il est acteur.**
kehl doh-mahzh'.	*eel eh tahk-tuhr'.*
What a pity!	He is an actor.

USE OF WORDS LIKE *ANYBODY* AND *ANYTHING*
(*The Indefinite Pronouns*, See 3.5; 3.1; 4.3)

Est-ce que quelqu'un est arrivé? Personne n'est arrivé.
            Personne n'est venu.
ehs' kuh kehl-kuhng' eh tah-ree-vay'?
            per-sohn' neh tah-reevay'. per-sohn' neh-vuh-new'.
Has anybody arrived? No one has arrived. Nobody has come.

Est-ce que quelqu'un a téléphoné? Quelqu'un a téléphoné.
ehs kuh kehl-kuhng ah tay-lay-foh-nay'? kehl-kuhng ah tay-lay-foh-nay'.
Has anybody called? Somebody called.

Avez-vous reçu des lettres? Oui, j'en ai reçu quelques-unes.
            Non, je n'en ai pas reçu.
ah-vay-voo' ruh-sew' deh lehtr'? Wee', zhah nay'ruh-sew' kehlk-zewn'.
            nohng, zhuh nahng nay pah ruh-sew'.
Have you received any letters? Yes, I received some.
            No, I haven't received any.

Avez-vous des revues américaines?
            Oui, j'en ai quelques-unes. En voilà une.
ah-vay-voo' deh ruh-vew zah-may-ree-kehn'?
            wee', zhahng nay' kehlk-zewn'. ahng vwah-lah' ewn.
Have you got any American magazines? Yes, I have some. There is one.

Avez-vous des journaux anglais? Je regrette mais je n'en ai pas.
ah-vay-voo' deh zhoor-noh' ahng-gleh'?
            zhuh ruh-greht' meh zhuh nahng nay pah'.
Have you got any English newspapers? I'm sorry. I don't have any.

Avez-vous une allumette? Non, je regrette.
ah-vay-voo' ewn ah-lew-meht? nohng, zhuh ruh-greht'.
Have you got a match? Sorry, I don't.

Est-ce qu'on vend du lait ici? Oui, on en vend.
  Donnez-m'en une bouteille.
ehs kohng vahng' dew leh' ee-see'?
    wee'. ohn ahng vahng'. doh-nay-mahng ewn boo-teh'-y.
Do you (they) sell milk here? Yes. We do. Please give me a bottle.

Avez-vous de l'argent? Non, je n'ai pas d'argent.
ah-vay-voo' duh lahr-zhahng'? nohng, zhuh nay pah dahr-zhahng'.
Have you got any money? No, I have no money.

Donnez-moi encore une bière. Donnez-moi une autre bière.
doh-nay-mwah' ahng-kohr' ewn byehr. doh-nay-mwah' ewn ohtr' byehr.
Give me another beer. Give me a different (brand of) beer.

Qu'avez-vous mangé? J'ai mangé du fromage.
kah-vay-voo mahng-zhay'? zhay mahng-zhay' dew froh-mahzh'.
What did you eat? I ate some cheese.

Qu'avez-vous acheté? J'ai acheté des robes et un tailleur.
kah-vay-voo zahsh-tay'? zhay ahsh-tay' deh rohb' ay uhng tah-yuhr'
What did you buy? I bought some dresses and a suit.

Qu'avez-vous fait? J'ai écouté des disques intéressants.
kah-vay-voo feh'? zhay ay-koo-tay' deh deesk zang-tay-reh-sahng.'
What did you do? I listened to some interesting records.

SENTENCES ON ADJECTIVES
(See 3.1, especially 3.1.d)

Hélène est plus grande que Marie.
ay-lehn' eh plew grahngd' kuh mah-ree'.
Helen is taller than Mary.

Alice est moins drôle qu'Irène.
ah-less' eh mwahng drohl kee-rehn'.
Alice is less humorous than Irene.

Agnès est aussi grande que Marie.
ah-nyehs' eht oh-see' grahngd kuh mah-ree'.
Agnes is as tall as Mary.

Anne n'est pas si grande que Marie.
ahn neh pah' see grahngd' kuh mah-ree'.
Ann is not so tall as Mary.

Françoise est la plus grande des filles.
frahng-swahz' eh lah plew grahngd' deh feey'.
Frances is the tallest of the girls.

Ce peintre a moins de talent. (See 1.5)
suh pang-tr ah mwahng duh tah-lahng'.
This painter has less talent.

Je prendrai un peu plus de viande.
zhuh prahng-dray' uhng puh plew' duh vyahngd'.
I will take a little more meat.

Prenez-en encore, je vous en prie.
pruh-nay-zahng ahng-kohr', zhuh voo zahng pree'.
Please have some more.

Je n'en veux pas davantage.
zhuh nahng vuh pah' dah-vahng-tahzh'.
I don't want any more.

Il ne peut plus y aller.
eel nuh puh plew zee ah-lay'.
He can no longer go there.

Ils ne veulent pas rester ici plus longtemps.
eel nuh vuhl pah reh-stay' ree-see' plew lohng-tahng'.
They don't want to stay here any longer.

La jeune fille avec la robe de soie bleue a été élue la reine du bal.
lah zhuhn feey ah-vehk lah rohb duh swah bluh.   (3.1.c; 8.1)
ah ay-tay ay-lew' lah rehn dew bahl'.
The girl with the blue silk dress was elected the queen of the ball.

Mon ami a acheté une nouvelle voiture rouge.
mohng ah-mee ah-ahsh-tay' ewn noo-vehl' vwah-tewr' roozh.
My friend bought a new red car.

Le vieux monsieur français n'est pas venu nous voir.
luh vyuh muh-syuh frahng-seh' neh pah vuh-new' noo vwahr'.
The old French gentleman didn't come to see us.

BASIC TYPES OF SENTENCES
(See 5.4; 8.7)

Affirmative: **Cette leçon est facile.**
seht luh-sohng' eh fah-seel'.
This lesson is easy.

Negative: **Cette leçon n'est pas difficile.**
seht luh-sohng' neh pah' dee-fee-seel'.
This lesson is not difficult.

Interrogative: **Est-ce que cette leçon est facile?**
eh's kuh seht luh-sohng' eh fah-seel'?
Is this lesson easy?

Elle est très facil
ehl-eh treh fah-se
It's very easy.

Cette pièce est grande, n'est-ce pas?
seht-pyehs' eh-grahng'-d, neh-s-pah'?
Isn't this room large?

Oui, elle est grand
wee, ehl-eh-grahng
Yes, it's large.

(See 4.1-2; 8.3; 8.6)

J'ai donné le livre à Jeanne.
zhay doh-nay' luh leevr' ah zhahn'.
I gave Jean the book.

Je l'ai donné à Thérèse.
zhuh lay doh-nay' ah tay-rehz'.
I gave it to Theresa.

Je le lui ai donné.
zhuh luh lwee ay doh-nay'.
I gave it to him.

Elle est allée là-bas.
ehl eh tah-lay' lah-bah'.
She went over there.

Est-il allé là-bas?
eh-teel ah-lay' lah-bah'?
Did he go over there?

Il n'y est pas allé.
eel nee eh pah zah-lay'.
He didn't go there.

Ne sont-ils pas allés là-bas?
nuh sohng-teel pah zah-lay' lah-bah'?
Didn't they go over there?

Oui, ils y sont allés.
wee, eel zee sohng tah-lay'.
Yes, they did.

Je veux aller à l'école.
zhuh vuh zah-lay' ah lay-kohl'.
I want to go to school.

Vous ne voulez pas aller à l'école.
voo nuh voo-lay pah zah-lay' ah lay-kohl'.
You don't want to go to school.

Qui veut aller à l'école?
kee vuh tah-lay' ah lay-kohl'?
Who wants to go to school?

Veulent-ils vraiment aller à l'école?
vuhl'-teel vreh-mahng ah-lay' ah lay-kohl'?
Do they really want to go to school?

Qui était la dame avec qui je vous ai vu hier soir? (See 4.8.)
kee ay-teh' lah dahm' ah-vehk kee zhuh voo zay vew' yehr swahr'?
Who was the lady with whom I saw you last night?

C'était ma tante qui vient d'arriver d'Europe.
say-teh' mah tahng't kee vyang dah-ree-vay' duh-rohp'.
She was my aunt who just came from Europe.

La jeune fille dont je vous parlais est sa fiancée.
lah zhuhn feey' dohng zhuh voo pahr-leh eh sah fee-ahng-say'.
The young lady of whom I was speaking is his fiancée.

La pendule qui est sur la cheminée est ancienne.
lah pahng-dewl' kee eh sewr lah shuh-mee-neh' eh tahng-syehn'.
The clock (which is) on the mantlepiece is an antique.

Les fauteuils que nous avons choisis sont modernes.
leh foh-tuh-eey' kuh noo zah-vohng shwah-zee' sohng moh-dehrn'.
The armchairs (that) we chose are modern.

A quoi pensez-vous?
ah kwah pahng-say voo'?
What are you thinking about?

Ne me dites pas que ce livre bleu ne vous appartient pas.
nuh muh deet pah' kuh suh leevr bluh' nuh voo-zah-pahr-tyang pah'.
Don't tell me that this blue book is not yours.

Quand elle est arrivée, il est parti. (See 8.4)
kahng tehl eh tah-ree-vay', eel-eh-pahr-tee'.
When she came, he left.

Si Jean vient, je lui en parlerai. (See 4.3 and 8.5.d)
see zhahng-vyang', zhuh lwee-ahng-pahr-luh-ray'.
If John comes, I will tell him about it.

Si Jean venait, je lui en parlerais.
see zhahng vuh-neh', zhuh lwee ahng pahr-luh-reh'.
If John came, I would tell him about it.

Si Jean était venu, je lui en aurais parlé.
see zhahng ay-teh vuh-new', zhuh lwee ahng oh-reh pahr-lay'.
If John had come, I would have told him about it.

Quand Jean viendra, je lui en parlerai.
kahng zhahng vyang-drah', zhuh lwee ahng pahr-luh-ray'.
When John comes, I will tell him about it.

Quand Jean est arrivé, je lui ai dit la nouvelle.
kahng zhahng eh tah-ree-vay', zhuh lwee ay dee lah noo-vehl'.
When John came, I told him the news.

(See 8.5; 6.2)

Il faut que je parte.
eel foh' kuh zhuh pahrt'.
I have to leave.

Attendez qu'il revienne.
ah-tahng-day keel ruh-vyehn'.
Wait until he returns.

Il faudra que la qualité soit meilleure.
eel foh-drah' kuh lah kah-lee-tay' swah meh-yuhr'.
The quality will have to be better.

Je regrette qu'il soit en retard.
zhuh ruh-greht' keel swah tahng ruh-tahr'.
I'm sorry he is late.

**Veuillez réserver votre place à l'avance, afin que
          (pour que) nous puissions vous la garantir.**
*vuh-yay ray-sehr-vay' vohtr plahs' ah lah-vahngs', ah-fang kuh
          (poor kuh) noo pwee-syohng voo lah gah-rahng-teer'.*
Please make your reservation in time so we can confirm it.

Dites-lui que le taxi est là.
deet-lwee kuh luh tahk-see eh lah'.
Tell him that the taxi is here.

Dites-lui qu'il vienne demain.
deet'-lwee keel vyehn duh-mang'
Tell him to come tomorrow.

C'est vrai, bien que cela vous paraisse étrange.
seh vreh', byang kuh suh-lah voo pah-rehs ay-trahngzh'.
It is true, although it may appear strange to you.

EVERYDAY CONVERSATIONS

BASIC EXPRESSIONS

Bonjour.
ohng-zhoor'.
Good morning. Hello.

Bonne nuit.
bohn nwee.
Good night.

Bonsoir.
bohng-swahr'.
Good evening. Good night.

Au revoir.
oh ruh-vwahr'
Goodbye.

Merci.
mehr-see'.
Thank you.

Il n'y a pas de quoi.
eel nee ah pah duh kwah'.
You're welcome.

Pardon.
par-dohng'.
Excuse me.

Combien?
kohng-bee-ang'?
How much?

S'il vous plaît.
seel voo pleh'.
Please.

Où?
oo?
Where?

Quand?
kahng?
When?

Je désire.
zhuh day-zeer'.
I want.

Donnez-moi.
doh-nay-mwah'.
Give me.

Où est le chat?
oo ay luh shah?
Where is the cat?

Je m'appelle Robert.
zhuh mah-pehl' roh-behr'.
My name is Robert.

Parlez-vous anglais?
pahr-lay-voo' zahng-glay'?
Do you speak English?

Je ne comprends pas.
zhuh nuh kohng-prahng' pah.
I don't understand.

Parlez plus lentement.
pahr-lay' plew lāhnt-mahng'.
Speak more slowly.

Comment allez-vous?
koh-mahn' tah-lay-voo'?
How do you do?

GETTING TO KNOW YOU

Bonjour, je suis le professeur Savant. **Je vous présente M. Entremont**
bohng-zhoor', zhuh swee luh *zhuh voo pray-zahnt' muh-syuh*
proh-fay-suhr sah-vahng'. *ahng-truh-mohng'.*
Good morning, I am professor Savant. May I present Mr. Entremont

Ma femme, Martine. **Et voici mon fils (ma fille).**
mah fahm', mahr-teen'. *ay vwah-see' mohng fees' (mah feey,*
This is my wife, Martine. And this is my son (daughter).

Je vois que vous parlez français.
zhuh vwah' kuh voo pahr-lay' frahng-say'.
You speak French, I see.

Un peu, mais mal, je crains.
uhng puh', may mahl', zhuh krang'.
A little, but quite poorly, I'm afraid.

Pouvez-vous comprendre ce que je dis?
poo-vay-voo' kohng-prahndr' suh kuh zhuh dee'?
Can you understand what I'm saying?

Est-ce votre premier voyage en France?
ehs vohtr pruh-myay' vwah-yazh' ahng frahngs?
Is this your first trip to France?

Oui, en effet. **Est-il agréable?**
wee, ahng ay-feh'. *eh-teel ah-gray-ah-bluh'?*
Yes, indeed. Are you enjoying yourself?

Beaucoup. J'aime le pays, surtout Paris.
boh-koo'. zhem luh pay-ee', sewr-too' pa-ree'.
Very much. I like the country, particularly Paris.

Où demeurez-vous aux Etats-Unis? **Je demeure à Chicago.**
oo duh-muh-ray-voo' oh zay-ta-zew-nee'? *zhuh duh-muhr' ah*
Where do you live in the United States? *shee-kah-goh'.*
I live in Chicago.

Si jamais vous passez par là, venez me voir.
see zha-may' voo pa-say' pahr-lah', vuh-nay' muh vwahr'.
If you ever come my way, call upon me.

Peut-être pourrions-nous déjeuner.
puh-tehtr' poo-ryohng-noo day-zhuh-nay'.
Perhaps we could have lunch.

Ou prendre un apéritif avant que vous partiez.
oo prahng-d'r uhn ah-pay-ree-teef' ah-vahng' kuh voo pahr-tyay'.
Or an aperitif before you leave.

COUNTING

(See **3.6** of the Grammar for a more complete treatment of numerals.)

Cardinal Numbers

un	**six**	**onze**	**seize**
uhng	*sees*	*ohngz*	*sehz*
one	six	eleven	sixteen
deux	**sept**	**douze**	**dix-sept**
duh	*seht*	*dooz*	*dee-seht*
two	seven	twelve	seventeen
trois	**huit**	**treize**	**dix-huit**
trwah	*weet*	*trehz*	*deez-weet*
three	eight	thirteen	eighteen
quatre	**neuf**	**quatorze**	**dix-neuf**
kahtr	*nuhf*	*kah-tohrz*	*deez-nuhf*
four	nine	fourteen	nineteen
cinq	**dix**	**quinze**	**vingt**
sangk	*dees*	*kangz*	*vang*
five	ten	fifteen	twenty

---

vingt et un	**cinquante**	**quatre-vingt-un**
vang-tay-uhng	*sang-kahngt*	*kahtr-vang-uhng*
twenty-one	fifty	eighty-one
vingt-deux	**soixante**	**quatre-vingt-dix**
vang-duh	*swah-sahngt*	*kahtr-vang-dees*
twenty-two	sixty	ninety
trente	**soixante-dix**	**quatre-vingt-onze**
trahngt	*swah-sahngt-dees*	*kahtr-vang-ohngz*
thirty	seventy	ninety-one
trente et un	**soixante et onze**	**cent**
trahngt-ay-uhng	*swah-sahngt-ay-ohngz*	*sahng*
thirty-one	seventy-one	one hundred
quarante	**quatre-vingts**	**mille**
kah-rahngt	*kahtr-vang*	*meel*
forty	eighty	one thousand

Ordinal Numbers and Fractions

The forms of the ordinal numbers are given in the Grammar (3.6), and the terms used for the fractions are identical, except in the case of ½, ⅓ and ¼.

½: *demi* (meaning "half," when no object is designated) and *la moitié* (when an object is designated). ⅓ is *le tiers.* ¼ is *le quart.*

quatre et demi
kahtr ay duh-mee'
four and a half

la moitié du revenu
lah mwah-tyay' dew ruh-vuh-new'
half the income

une pomme et demie
ewn pohm ay duh-mee'
an apple and a half

deux moitiés
duh mwah-tyay'
two halves

le tiers, le quart et le dixième de la somme
luh tyehr, luh kahr ay luh dee-zyehm' duh lah sohm
a third, a fourth (a quarter) and a tenth of the sum

THE CLOCK AND THE CALENDAR

Quelle heure est-il?
kehl uhr eh-teel'?
What time is it?

Il est dix heures.
ee leh dee zuhr'.
It is ten o'clock.

Il est trois heures et quart (et demie) (quatre heures moins le quart).
eel eh trwah zuhr ay kahr' (ay duh-mee') (kah-truhr' mwahng luh kahr)
It is quarter (half) past three (a quarter to four).

Les jours de la semaine sont: lundi, mardi, mercredi, jeudi, vendredi, samedi, dimanche.
leh zhoor duh lah suh-mehn' sohng: luhng-dee', mahr-dee', mehr-kruh-dee', zhuh-dee', vahng-druh-dee', sahm-dee', dee-mahngsh'.
The days of the week are: Monday, Tuesday, Wednesday, Thursday, Friday, Saturday, Sunday.

Les mois de l'année sont: janvier, février, mars, avril, mai, juin, juillet, août, septembre, octobre, novembre, décembre.
leh mwah duh lah-nay' sohng: zhahng-vee-ay', fayv-ree-ay', mahrs, ah-vreel', meh, zhew-ang', zhwee-yeh', oo, sehp-tahng'-br, ohk-toh'-br, noh-vahng'-br, day-sahng'-br.
The months of the year are: January, February, March, April, May, June, July, August, September, October, November, December.

Les saisons de l'année sont le printemps, l'été, l'automne, l'hiver.
leh seh-zohng' duh lah-nay' sohng luh prang-tahng', lay-tay', loh-tohn'.
lee-vehr'.
The seasons of the year are spring, summer, autumn, winter.

Ce matin (Cet après-midi) le soleil brillait.
suh mah-tang' (seh tah-preh-mee-dee') luh soh-leh'-eey bree-yeh'.
This morning (afternoon) the sun was shining.

Quel temps fait-il?	**Il fait un temps superbe.**
kehl tahng feh-teel'?	*eel feh-tuhng tahng sew-pehrb'.*
How is the weather?	It is a beautiful day.
Il pleut (neige).	**Il pleut à verse.**
eel pluh (nehzh).	*eel pluh' ah vehrs'.*
It is raining (snowing).	It is pouring.

Quels sont les principaux jours fériés en France?
kehl sohng leh prang-see-poh' zhoor fay-ree-ay' ahng frahngs'?
What are the most important holidays in France?

**Le jour de l'An, le lundi de Pàques, le 1er mai (Fête du Travail), l'Ascen-
sion, le lundi de Pentecôte, le 14 juillet (Fête nationale), l'Assomp-
tion (15 août), la Toussaint, le 11 novembre (Armistice) et Noël.**
*luh zhoor duh lahng', luh luhng-dee duh pahk', luh pruh-myehr meh
(feht dew trah-vahy'), lah-sahng-syohng', luh luhng-dee duh pahng't-
koht', luh kah-tohrz zhwee-yeh' (feht nah-syoh-nahl'), lah-sohnp-
syohng' (kanz oo'), lah too-sang', luh ohngz noh-vahng-b'r
(ahr-mee-stees') ay noh-ehl.*
New Year's, Easter Monday, May 1st (Labor Day), Ascension, Whitmon-
day, July 14th, Assumption, All Saints', Armistice and Christmas.

STRANGER IN TOWN

Y a-t-il quelqu'un ici qui parle anglais?
ee-ah-teel kehlk-uhng ee-see' kee pahrl ahng-gleh'?
Is there anyone here who speaks English?

J'ai perdu mon chemin.	**Où voulez-vous aller?**
zhay pehr-dew' mohng shuh-mang'.	*oo voo-lay-voo-zah-lay?*
I've lost my way.	Where do you want to go?
Me comprenez-vous?	**Non, je ne vous comprends pas.**
nuh kohng-pruh-nay'-voo?	*nohng, zhuh nuh voo kohng-prahng' pah.'*
Do you understand me?	No, I don't understand you.

Parlez plus lentement, s'il vous plaît.
ahr-lay' plew lahng-t-mahng', seel-voo-pleh'.
Please speak more slowly.

Veuillez répéter.
vuh-ee-yay' ray-pay-tay'.
Please repeat.

Que dites-vous?
kuh deet voo?
What are you saying?

Je ne peux pas trouver mon portefeuille.
zhuh nuh puh pah troo-vay' mohng pohr-tuh-fuh-eey'.
I can't find my wallet.

On m'a volé!
ohng mah voh-lay'!
I've been robbed!

Appelez la police (s'il vous plaît)!
ah-puh-lay' lah poh-lees' (seel-voo-pleh').
(Please) call the police!

Où est le commissariat de police?
oo eh luh koh-mee-sah-ree-ah' duh poh-lees'?
Where is the Police Station?

Par là.
pahr-lah'.
That way.

Au secours!
oh suh-koor'!
Help!

Au feu!
oh fuh'!
Fire!

Pouvez-vous m'aider?
poo-vay'-voo meh-day'?
Can you help me?

Je suis américain (américaine).
zhuh swee ah-may-ree-kang' (ah-may-ree-kehn').
I am an American.

Conduisez-moi au consulat américain.
kohng-dwee-zay-mwah oh kohng-sew-lah' ah-may-ree-kang'.
Take me to the American consulate.

J'ai laissé mon pardessus dans le train.
zhay leh-say' mohng pahr-duh-sew' dahng luh trang.
I've left my overcoat on the train.

Comment pourrai-je le retrouver?
koh-mahng' poo-rayzh luh ruh-troo-vay?
How can I get it back?

Je voudrais téléphoner.
zhuh voo-dreh' tay-lay-foh-nay'.
I would like to use the phone.

Etes-vous blessé?
ayt-voo bleh-say'?
Are you hurt?

Je ne sais plus où est mon hôtel?
zhuh nuh seh plew oo eh mohng oh-tehl'?
I don't remember where my hotel is.

J'ai perdu mon parapluie.
zhay pehr-dew' mohng pah-rah-plwee'.
I've lost my umbrella.

Pouvez-vous m'indiquer où se trouve le bureau des objets trouvés?
*poo-vay-voo mang-dee-kay' oo suh troov luh bew-roh'
    deh zohb-zheh' troo-vay'?*
Can you tell me where the lost and found office is?

Laissez-moi tranquille ou j'appelle un agent.
leh-say mwah trahng-keel oo zhah-pehl uhng ah-zhahng'.
Don't bother me or I will call a policeman.

Où m'emmenez-vous?   **Je veux un avocat.**
oo mahng-muh-nay'-voo?   *zhuh vuh uhng ah-voh-kah'.*
Where are you taking me?   I need a lawyer.

Au commissariat de police. Vous êtes en état d'arrestation.
*oh koh-mee-sah-ree-ah' duh poh-lees'. voo-zeht' ahn ay-tah'
        dah-rehs-tah-syohng'.*
To the police station. You are under arrest.

Voulez-vous me donner votre nom et votre addresse?
voo-lay-voo muh doh-nay' vohtr nohng ay vohtr ah-drehs'?
Will you give me your name and address?

Montrez-moi votre permis de conduire.
mohng-tray'- mwah vohtr pehr-mee' duh kohng-dweer'.
Let me see your driver's license.

Quel est le nom de votre compagnie d'assurances?
kehl eh luh nohng duh vohtr kohng-pah-nyee' dah-sew-rahngs'?
What is the name of your insurance company?

Votre voiture est-elle très endommagée?
vohtr vwah-tewr' et-tehl tray zahng-doh-mah-zhay'?
Is your car badly damaged?

J'ai perdu mon permis de séjour.
zhay pehr-dew' mohng pehr-mee' duh say-zhoor'.
I have lost my tourist card.

Puis-je en avoir un autre?
pweezh ahng ah-vwahr' uhng ohtr?
Can I get a replacement?

J'ai perdu une valise.   **Elle porte les initiales R. D. C.**
zhai pehr-dew' ewn vah-leez'.   el pohrt lay zee-nee-syahl' ehr. deh. seh.
I have lost a suitcase.   It carries the initials R. D. C.

En avez-vous trouvé une correspondant à cette description?
*ahng ah-vay-voo troo-vay ewn koh-rehs-pohng-dahng ah seht
        dehs-kreep-syohng'?*
Have you found one answering that description?

Si on vous la rapporte, téléphonez-moi à GOBelins 70-56.
*see ohng voo lah rah-pohrt', tay-lay-foh-nay-mwah' ah goh-blang'
        swah-sahngt-dees'—sang-kahngt-sees'.*
If it comes in, telephone me at GObelins 70-56.

ABOARD SHIP

Je voyage en classe cabine. Cabine numéro 465.
zhuh vwah-yahzh' ahng klahs ka-been'. kah-been' new-may-ro' kahtr-sahngt-swah-sahngt-sang'.
I am traveling cabin class. Stateroom No. 465.

Pouvez-vous me montrer le chemin, s'il vous plaît?
poo-vay-voo' muh mohng-tray' luh shuh-mang', seel-voo-pleh'.
Can you please direct me?

Apportez nos bagages à notre cabine.
ah-pohr-tay' noh bah-gahzh' ah nohtr kah-been'.
Take our bags to our cabin.

A quelle heure sert-on le déjeuner?
ah kel uhr sairt-ohng' luh day-zhuh-nay'?
What time is lunch served?

Je voudrais louer un transat.
zhuh voo-dreh loo-ay' uhng trahng-zaht'.
I would like to rent a deck chair.

Combien coûte un transat?
kohng-bee-ang' koot uhng trahng-zaht'?
How much does a deck chair cost?

Ça coûte 500 francs.
sa koot sang-sahng frahng'.
The cost is 500 francs.

Avez-vous un remède contre le mal de mer?
ah-vay-voo uhng ruh-mehd' kohng-t'r luh mahl duh mehr?
Do you have anything for seasickness?

A quelle heure le bateau sera-t-il à quai?
a kehl uhr' luh bah-toh' suh-rah-teel' ah-keh'?
At what time does the boat dock tomorrow?

PLANE TRAVEL

Y a-t-il un avion pour Bruxelles?
ee-ya-teel' uhng ah-vee-ohng ' poor Brew-sehl'?
Is there a plane for Brussels?

Je voudrais réserver une place sur le prochain avion.
zhuh voo-dreh' ray-zehr-vay ewn plahs' sewr luh proh-shang ah-vee-ohng'.
I'd like to reserve a seat on the next flight.

Une place près du hublot, s'il vous plaît.
ewn plahs preh dew ew-bloh', seel voo pleh'.
A seat next to the window, please.

Qu'avez-vous à boire?
kah-vay-voo' zah bwahr?
What do you have to drink?

L'avion arrivera-t-il à l'heure?
lah-vee-ohng ah-ree-vrah-teel ah luhr'?
Will the plane arrive on time?

L'avion n'a pas encore décollé.
lah-vee-ohng nah pah zahng-kohr day-koh-lay'.
The plane has not taken off yet.

L'avion vient d'atterrir.
lah-vee-ohng vyang dah-teh-reer'.
The plane just landed.

Comment s'appelle l'aéroport de Paris?
koh-mahng' sa-pel' la-ay-roh-pohr' duh pa-ree'?
What is the name of the Paris airport?

Il y en a deux, Orly et le Bourget.
eel ee ahng ah duh, or-lee' ay luh boor-zhay'.
There are two—Orly and Bourget.

Combien de temps faut-il pour aller de l'aéroport à Paris?
*kohng-byang' duh tahng foh-teel' poor ah-lay' duh
    lah-ay-roh-pohr ah pah-ree'?*
How long does it take from the airport to Paris?

A peu près trente minutes.
ah puh preh trahnt mee-newt'.
Approximately thirty minutes.

ALL ABOARD

A quelle heure part le prochain train pour Toulouse?
ak kehl uhr par luh proh-shang' trang poor too-looz'?
When is the next train for Toulouse?

A quelle heure arrive-t-il?
ah kel uhr a-reev-teel'?
When does it arrive?

Combien coûte le billet?
kohng-bee-ang' koot luh bee-yay'?
What is the fare?

Est-ce un express ou un omnibus?
ehs uhn eks-pres' oo uhn ohm-nee-bews'?
Is it an express or a local?

Un billet pour Lille.
uhng bee-yay' poor leel.
One ticket to Lille.

Première classe.	**Deuxième classe.**	**Aller.**	**Aller-retour.**
pruh-myair' klahs'.	*duh-zyem' klahs'.*	*a-lay'.*	*a-lay' ruh-tour'.*
First class.	Second class.	One way.	Round trip.

J'aimerais réserver une place.
zhai-muh-ray' ray-zehr-vay' ewn plahs'.
I'd like to reserve a seat.

Cette place, est-elle prise?
set plahs, ay-tel preez?
Is this seat taken?

En voiture, s'il vous plaît.
ahng vwah-tewr', seel-voo-play'
All aboard (please).

Attention au départ.
ah-tahng-syohng' oh day-pahr'.
Train leaving.

Quai deux, voie quatre.
kay-duh, vwah kah'-tr.
Platform 2, track 4.

Où est le wagon-restaurant?
oo ay luh vah-gohng-ray-stoh-rahng'?
Where is the dining-car?

Contrôle des billets, messieurs dames, s'il vous plaît.
kohng-trohl' deh bee-yeh', meh-syuh-dahm', seel-voo-pleh'.
Tickets, please, ladies and gentlemen.

Quand arrive-t-on à Paris?
kahng tah-reev-tohng ah pah-ree'?
How soon do we arrive at Paris?

GOING THROUGH CUSTOMS

Ouvrez vos bagages, s'il vous plaît.
oo-vray' vo ba-gahzh' seel voo play'.
Open your baggage, please.

Avez-vous autre chose que des vêtements?
a-vay-voo' zohtr shohz kuh day veht-mahng'?
Have you anything but wearing apparel?

Oui, quelques articles de toilette.
wee, kel-kuh' zar-teekl' duh twah-leht'.
Yes, a few toilet articles.

Et mon appareil photographique.
ay mohng a-pa-ray' fo-to-gra-feek'.
And my camera.

Est-ce pour votre usage personnel?
ehs' poor vohtr ew-zahzh pehr-soh-nehl'?
Is it for personal use?

Oui, monsieur.
wee, m-syuh'.
Yes, it is.

Combien de cigarettes avez-vous?
kohng-bee-ang' duh see-gahr-et' a-vay-voo'?
How many cigarettes do you have?

La machine à écrire, est-elle pour vendre?
la mah-sheen' ah ay-kreer', ay-tel' poor vahndr?
Is the typewriter for sale?

Non, c'est pour mon usage personnel.
nohng, seh poor mohng ew-zahzh' pehr-soh-nehl'.
No, it is for my personal use.

Veuillez porter ces bagages au train de Paris.
vuh-yay' pohr-tay' seh ba-gahzh' oh trang duh pa-ree'.
Please take these bags to the Paris train.

GETTING AROUND TOWN

Taxis

Taxi!   **Etes-vous libre?**
tahk-see'!   *eht'-voo leebr?*
Taxi!   Are you free?

Conduisez-moi à l'Hôtel Georges V (à la gare).
kohng-dwee-zay'-mwah ah loh-tehl zhohrzh sangk' (ah lah gahr).
Take me to the Hotel George V (to the station).

Arrêtez au coin.   **C'est près de l'Etoile.**
ah-reh-tay' oh kwahng.   *seh preh duh lay-twahl'.*
Stop at the corner.   It is near (the) Etoile.

Combien de pourboire doit-on donner au chauffeur?
kohng-byang' duh poor-bwahr' dwah-tohng doh-nay' oh shoh-fuhr'?
What tip should one give the driver?

Déposez-nous de l'autre côté de la place.
day-poh-zay-noo' duh loh'-tr koh-tay' duh lah plahs'.
Let us out at the other side of the square.

Quel est le prix de la course?
kehl eh luh pree duh lah koors'?
How much is the fare?

Le prix est indiqué au compteur.
luh pree eh tang-dee-kay' oh kohng-tuhr'.
The price (fare) shows on the meter.

Métro (Subway)

Je voudrais un ticket de seconde.
zhuh voo-dreh' uhng tee-keh' duh suh-gohnd'.
I want one second-class ticket.

Je voudrais un carnet de premières.
zhuh voo-dreh' uhng kar-nay' duh pruh-myehr.
I want a book of first class tickets.

C'est combien?
seh kohng-byang'?
How much is it?

Où est le quai?
oo ay' luh kay'?
Where is the platform?

Buses

Donnez-moi un carnet.
doh-nay-mwah' uhng kar-nay'.
Let me have a book of tickets.

Je vais à Montparnasse.
zhuh veh zah mohng-pahr-nahs'.
I am going to Montparnasse.

Une correspondance, s'il vous plaît.
ewn koh-rehs-pohng-dahns', seel-voo-pleh'.
A transfer, please.

Combien?
kohng-bee-ang'?
How much is it?

Faites-moi savoir quand nous arrivons à la Madeleine.
fet-mwah' sa-vwahr' kahng noo za-ree-vohng' zah lah mahd-lehn'.
Let me know when we get to La Madeleine.

Jusqu'à quelle heure marchent les autobus sur cette ligne?
zhews-kah' kel uhr mahrsh' leh zoh-toh-bews' sewr set leen'yuh?
How late does this line operate?

Bateaux Mouches

Donnez-moi un billet pour tout le trajet.
doh-nay-mwah uhng bee-yeh' poor too luh trah-zheh'.
Give me a ticket for the full ride.

A quelle heure part le prochain bateau?
ah kehl uhr pahr luh proh-shang' ba-toh'?
What time does the next boat leave?

Combien coûtent les billets pour les enfants?
kohng-bee-ang' koot lay bee-yay' poor leh zahng-fahng'?
How much are tickets for children?

MOTORING THROUGH FRANCE

Où est le poste à essence le plus proche?
oo ay' luh pohst ah ay-sahns' luh plew prohsh?
Where is the nearest gas station?

Faites-le plein.
feht' luh plang'.
Fill the tank. (Fill'er up.)

Un litre d'huile.
uhng leetr dweel.
A liter of oil.

Vérifiez l'huile, l'eau, et les accus.
vay-ree-fyay' lweel', loh, ay leh zah-kew'.
Check the oil, water, and battery.

Est-ce la route de Nancy?
ehs la root duh nahng-see'?
Is this the road to de Nancy?

Tout droit à 6 kilomètres.
too drwah' ah see kee-loh-mehtr'.
Straight ahead at 6 kilometers.

Tournez à gauche (à droite) au prochain croisement.
toor-nay' ah gohsh' (ah drwaht) oh proh-shang' krwahz-mahng'.
Turn left (right) at the next crossroad.

Pouvons-nous arriver à Nice avant la nuit?
poo-vohng-noo' zah-ree-vay ah nees a-vahng' la nwee?
Can we reach Nice before nightfall?

Mes phares ne marchent pas.
may fahr' nuh marsh pah.
My lights don't work.

J'ai un pneu crevé.
zhai uhng pnuh kruh-vay'.
I have a flat tire.

Où peut-on faire une réparation?
oo' puh-tohng fehr ewn ray-pah-rah-syohng'?
Where can I have repairs done?

Quelle ville est-ce?
kehl veel ehs?
What town is this?

Envoyez quelqu'un pour réparer ma voiture.
ahng-vwah-yay' kel-kuhng' poor ray-pah-ray' mah vwah-tewr'.
Send someone to repair my car.

Conduisez-moi au garage le plus proche, s'il vous plaît.
kohng-dwee-zay-mwah oh gah-razh luh plew prohsh', seel-voo-pleh'.
Please take me to the nearest garage.

Pouvez-vous pousser ma voiture?
poo-vay-voo' poo-say' ma vwah-tewr'?
Can you give my car a push?

Pouvez-vous m'emmener à Grenoble?
poo-vay voo mem-muh-nay ah gruh-nohb'l?
Can you give me a lift to Grenoble?

AUTO CARE

Je suis en panne.
zhuh swee zahng pahn.
My car has broken down.

Où est le garage le plus proche?
oo eh luh gah-razh' luh plew prohsh?
Where is the nearest garage?

Voulez-vous vérifier les pneus?
voo-lay-voo' vay-ree-fee-ay' leh pnuh?
Please check the tires.

Combien coûte le litre d'essence?
kohng-byang' koot luh leetr deh-sahngs'?
What is the price of gasoline per liter?

Donnez-moi 20 litres.
doh-nay-mwah' vang leetr'.
Give me 20 liters.

Veuillez faire le plein d'essence.
vuh-yay fehr luh plang deh-sahngs'.
Please fill it up.

Veuillez changer l'huile.
vuh-yay' shahng-zhay' lweel.
Please change the oil.

Veuillez graisser la voiture.
vuh-yay' greh-say' lah vwah-tewr'.
Please grease the car.

Ajustez les freins, s'il vous plaît.
ah-zhew-stay' leh frang, seel-voo-pleh'.
Please adjust the brakes.

Veuillez mettre de l'eau dans le radiateur.
vuh-yay' mehtr duh-loh dahng luh rah-dee-ah-tuhr'.
Please put water in the radiator.

L'engrenage ne fonctionne pas bien.
lahng-gruh-nahzh' nuh fohngk-syohn' pàh byang.
There is something wrong with the gears.

Veuillez envoyer une voiture de dépannage.
vuh-yay' ahng-vwah-yay' ewn vwah-tewr duh day-pah-nahzh'.
Please send a tow car.

Y a-t-il un mécanicien ici qui connaisse les voitures américaines?
ee-ah-teel uhng may-kah-nee-syang ee-see' kee koh-nehs' leh vwah-tewr' ah-may-ree-kehn'.
Is there a mechanic here who knows American cars?

Combien de temps prendra la réparation?
kohng-byang duh tahng prahng-drah' lah ray-pah-rah-syohng'?
How long will the repairs take?

Accélérateur.	**Pare-chocs.**	**Embrayage.**	**Moteur.**
ah-ksay-lay-rah-tuhr'.	*pahr-shohk'.*	*ahng-breh-yahzh'.*	*moh-tuhr'.*
Accelerator.	Bumper.	Clutch.	Engine.
Phare (ampoule).	**Allumage.**	**Démarreur.**	**Pare-brise.**
fahr (ahng-pool').	*ah-lew-mahzh'.*	*day-mah-ruhr'.*	*pahr-breez'.*
Headlight (bulb).	Ignition.	Starter.	Windshield.

TRAFFIC SIGNS AND DIRECTIONS

Stationnement interdit.	**Sens unique.**	**Carrefour.**
stah-syohn-mahng' ang-tehr-dee'.	*sahng-sew-neek'.*	*kahr-foor'.*
No parking.	One way.	Crossroads.
Passage à niveau.	**Passage interdit.**	**Ecole.**
pah-sahzh' ah nee-voh'.	*pah-sahzh' ang-tehr-dee'.*	*ay-kohl'.*
Level crossing.	No thoroughfare.	School.

Hôpital, silence. **Défense de tourner à droite (gauche).**
oh-pee-tahl', see-lahngs'. *day-fahng'-s duh toor-nay' ah drwaht (gohsh).*
Hospital, quiet. No right (left) turn.

Détour.	**Route barrée.**	**Ralentissez.**
day-toor'.	*root bah-ray'.*	*rah-lahng-tee-say'.*
Detour.	Road closed.	Slow down.

Connaissez-vous un hôtel où je puisse passer la nuit?
koh-neh-say voo uhng oh-tehl' oo zhuh pwees pah-say lah nwee'?
Do you know a hotel where I can stay overnight?

Sommes-nous sur la route de Genève? **Oui, tout droit.**
sohm-noo sewr lah root duh zhuh-nehv'? *wee, too drwah.*
Are we on the road to Geneva? Yes, straight ahead.

Faites demi-tour et retournez à Orléans. **A droite (gauche).**
feht duh-mee-toor' ay ruh-toor-nay' zah ohr-lay- *ah-drwaht' (gohsh).*
Turn around and return to Orleans. *ahng'.* To the right (left).

Virage dangereux. **Avez-vous une carte routière?**
vee-rahzh dahng-zhuh-ruh'. *ah-vay-voo ewn kahrt roo-tyehr'?*
Dangerous curve. Do you have a road map?

AT THE HOTEL

Avez-vous une chambre de réservée à mon nom?
ah-vay-voo ewn shahmbr duh ray-zehr-vay ah mohng nohng'?
Have you a room reserved for me?

Avez-vous une chambre à un lit (à deux lits)?
a-vay-voo' zewn shahmbr' ah uhng (duh) lee?
Have you a single (double) room?

Je désire une chambre avec salle de bains.
zhuh day-zeer ewn shahmbr ah-vehk sahl duh bang'.
I want a room with bath.

Quel est le prix?　　**Y compris service et taxes?**
kel ay luh pree?　　*ee kohng-pree' sehr-vees' ay tahx?*
What is the price?　　Does that include service and tax?

Je voudrais une chambre plus petite (plus grande).
zhuh voo-dreh zewn shahmbr plew puh-teet (plew grahnd).
I want a smaller (larger) room.

Oui, cette chambre ira.　　**Faites monter mes bagages, s'il vous plaît.**
wee, set shahmbr ee-ra'.　　*feht mohng-tay may ba-gahzh', seel-voo-pleh'.*
Yes, this room will do.　　Please have my bags carried up.

Voulez-vous remplir la fiche d'inscription?
voo-lay-voo' rahng-pleer' la-feesh' dang-screep-syohng'?
Would you please sign the registration blank.

Y a-t-il des toilettes à cet étage?
ee-a-teel' deh twah-leht ah set ay-tahzh'?
Is there a lavatory on this floor?

Où est la salle de bain?　　**Je voudrais prendre un bain.**
oo ay lah sahl duh bang'?　　*zhuh voo-drai' phahndr uhng bang.*
Where is the bathroom?　　I wish to take a bath.

Apportez-moi d'autres cintres.
a-pohr-tay-mwah dohtr sangtr.
Bring me some more coat-hangers.

Pourriez-vous me repasser une robe?
poo-ryay-voo' muh ruh-pah-say' ewn rohb?
Could you press a dress for me?

J'en aurai besoin à 6 heures.
zhahng oh-reh buh-zwang' ah seez uhr'.
I will need it back at 6 o'clock.

Je voudrais être réveillé à 7 heures.
zhuh voo-dreh zehtr ray-veh-yay' ah seht uhr.
I wish to be called at 7 o'clock.

Faites-moi monter le petit déjeuner à 8 heures.
feht-mwah mohng-tay' luh puh-tee day-zhuh-nay' ah weet uhr'.
Have breakfast sent up at 8 o'clock.

Je voudrais du café et des croissants.
zhuh voo-dreh dew kah-fay' ay day krwah-sahng'.
I wish to have coffee and rolls.

Je vais faire une excursion à Chartres.
zhuh veh fehr ewn eks-kewr-syohng' ah shahrtr'.
I am going on a trip to Chartres.

Puis-je laisser une partie de mes bagages ici?
pweezh leh-say ewn par-tee duh may ba-gahzh ee-see'?
May I leave some of my baggage here?

Je serai de retour le 17.
zhuh suh-ray duh ruh-tour' luh dees-seht.
I will be back on the 17th.

Je pars demain. Préparez ma note, s'il vous plaît.
zhuh par duh-mang'. pray-pa-ray' ma noht', seel-voo-pleh'.
I am leaving tomorrow. Please draw up my bill.

Je prends le train de 9 heures.
zhuh prahng luh trang duh nuhv uhr.
I am taking the 9 o'clock train.

Voudriez-vous m'appeler un taxi.
voo-dree-ay-voo mah-puh-lay uhng tahk-see'.
Would you have a taxi ready for me.

RENTING A ROOM

Une chambre sans salle de bains.
ewn shahmbr sahng sahl duh bang'.
A room without bath.

Je resterai ici deux semaines.
zhuh rehs-tuh-ray ee-see duh suh-mehn'.
I will be staying here for two weeks.

Prenez tous les messages.
pruh-nay' too lay meh-sahzh'.
Take all messages.

Je prendrai mon déjeuner ailleurs.
zhuh prahng-dray' mohng day-zhuh-nay' ah-yuhr'.
I will eat my noon meal elsewhere.

Et occupez-vous de mon courrier, s'il vous plaît.
ay oh-kew-pay-voo' duh mohng koo-ree-ay', seel-voo-play'.
And look after my mail, please.

Si des amis me demandent, faites-les monter.
see day zah-mee' muh duh-mahnd', feht-lay' mohng-tay'.
If friends call, show them up.

THE SIDEWALK CAFÉ

Garçon!
gahr-sohng'!
Waiter!

Une bière, s'il vous plaît.
ewn byehr, seel-voo-pleh'.
A beer, please.

Un citron pressé pour madame.
uhng see-trohng' preh-say' poor mah-dahm'.
Lemonade for the lady.

Un verre de cherry.
uhng vehr duh sheh-ree'.
A glass of sherry.

Une orangeade et des gâteaux pour les enfants.
ewn oh-rahng-zhahd' ay deh gah-toh' poor leh zahng-fahng'.
An orangeade and pastry for the children.

Un whisky.
uhng wees-kee'.
A whisky.

Une bouteille d'eau minérale.
ewn boo-teh-eey doh mee-nay-rahl'.
A bottle of mineral water.

Qu'avez-vous comme jus de fruit? Nous avons du jus d'orange, de tomate et de pamplemousse.
kah-vay-voo kohm zhew duh frwee? noo zah-vohng dew zhew doh-rahngzh', duh toh-maht' ay duh pahng-pluh-moos'.
What kind of fruit juices do you have? We have orange, tomato and grapefruit.

Quelles liqueurs avez-vous? Nous avons de la Bénédictine, du Cointreau et du Grand Marnier.
kehl lee-kuhr ah-vay-voo? noo zah-vohng duh lah bay-nay-deek-teen', dew kwahng-troh' ay dew grahng mahr-nyay'.
What kind of liqueurs do you have? We have Benedictine, Cointreau and Grand Marnier.

Un verre de vin rouge (blanc).
uhng vehr duh vang roozh (blahng).
A glass of red (white) wine.

L'addition, s'il vous plaît.
lah-dee-syohng', seel-voo-pleh'.
The check, please.

Le service, est-il compris dans l'addition? Non, Monsieur (Madame).
luh sehr-vees, eh-teel   kohng-pree   dahng lah-dee-syohng'? nohng,
*   m-syuh' (mah-dahm').*
Is the service included in the bill? No, it is not.

DINING OUT

Pouvez-vous me recommander un bon restaurant?
poo-vay-voo' muh ruh-koh-mahng-day' uhng bohng   rehs-toh-rahng'?
Can you recommend a good restaurant?

Je voudrais réserver une table pour huit heures.
zhuh voo-dreh ray-zehr-vay' ewn tahbl poor weet uhr'.
I would like to reserve a table for 8 o'clock.

Garçon, le menu, s'il vous plaît.
gar-sohng', luh muh-new' seel-voo-pleh'.
Waiter, a menu please.

Quelle est la spécialité de la maison?
kel ay la spay-see-ah-lee-tay' duh la may-zohng'?
What is the specialty of the house?

En quoi consiste ce plat?   **Que recommandez-vous?**
ahng kwah kohng-seest suh plah?   *kuh ruh-koh-mahng-day-voo'?*
What does this dish consist of?   What do you recommend?

Merci, mais ce plat est beaucoup trop cher.
mehr-see , meh suh plah ay boh-koo troh shehr'.
Thank you, but this dish is far too expensive.

Recommandez-moi quelque chose de plus simple et de moins cher.
ruh-koh-mahng-day-mwah' kel-kuh shohz duh plew sangpl ay duh
*   mwahng shehr'.*
Please suggest something simpler and less expensive.

Apportez-moi une carafe d'eau glacée.
a-pohr-tay-mwah' ewn ka-rahf doh glah-say'.
Bring me a pitcher of ice water.

Un verre d'eau naturelle, s'il vous plaît.
uhng vehr' doh na-tew-rel', seel-voo-pleh'.
A glass of plain water, please.

Pour commencer, nous prendrons du potage.
poor koh-mahng-say, noo prahng-drohng dew poh-tahzh'.
To start, we'll have soup.

Encore du beurre.   **Et apportez-nous du café, s'il vous plaît.**
ahng-kor' dew buhr.   *ay ah-pohr-tay noo dew kah-fay', seel-voo-pleh'.*
More butter.   And please bring us some coffee.

Puis-je voir la carte des vins, s'il vous plaît?
pweezh vwahr la kahrt day vang, seel-voo-pleh'?
May I see the wine list, please?

Une demi-carafe de vin rouge ordinaire.
ewn duh-mee' ka-rahf' duh vang roozh' or-dee-nehr'.
A half carafe of ordinary red wine.

Prenons ceci comme dessert.   **Le service était excellent.**
pruh-nohng' suh-see kohm day-sayr'.   *luh ser-vees' ay-teh' tex-say-lahng'.*
Let us have this for dessert.   The service was excellent.

Il me semble qu'il y a une erreur dans l'addition.
eel muh sahng-bl keel ee ah ewn eh-ruhr dahng lah-dee-syohng'.
I think you've added up this bill incorrectly.

Vous avez raison. J'ai fait une erreur.
voo-za-vay reh-zohng'. zheh feh ewn eh-ruhr.
You are right. I've made an error.

Nous avons trouvé le repas très bon.
noo zah-vohng troo-vay luh ruh-pah treh bohng'.
We enjoyed the meal very much.

EAT LIKE THE FRENCH

Beignets (aux pommes).
beh-nyeh' (oh pohm').
Apple fritters.

Bifteck aux pommes frites.
beef-tehk' oh pohm-freet'.
Steak with French fried potatoes.

Bouillabaisse.
boo-yah-behs'.
Soup made of different types of fish and spiced with garlic, saffron, tomato, olive oil; specialty of Provence.

Brioche.
bree-ohsh'.
Breakfast roll made of flour, butter and eggs.

Canard à l'orange.
kah-nahr ah loh-rahng zh'.
Roast duck with orange sauce.

Châteaubriant.
shah-toh-bree-ahng'.
Thick grilled steak.

Choucroute garnie.
shoo-kroot' gahr-nee'.
Sauerkraut with ham, frankfurters, salt pork sausage; specialty of
    Strasbourg.

Coq au vin.
kohk oh vang'.
Chicken cooked in a red wine sauce.

Coquille St.-Jacques.
koh-keey sang-zhahk'.
Scallops cooked in the shell with a Béchamel sauce.

Crêpes Suzette.
krehp sew-zeht'.
Thin wheat pancakes rolled with jelly and served with liquor sauce
    in flames.

Croissant.
krwah-sahng'.
Crescent-shaped, crisp breakfast roll made of flour, butter and eggs.

Entrecôte Bercy. *ahng-truh-koht behr-see'.* Sirloin steak with wine sauce.	**Escargots.** *ehs-kahr-goh'.* Snails.
Filet de sole meunière. *fee-leh duh sohl muh-nyehr'.* Filets of sole fried in butter.	**Fonds d'artichaut.** *fohng dahr-tee-shoh'.* Artichoke hearts.

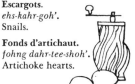

Gigot de mouton pré-salé.
zhee-goh' duh moo-tohng' pray sah-lay'.
Leg of lamb; specialty of northwestern France.

**Omelette (au jambon) (Parmentier) (aux champignons) (aux fines
    herbes) (au fromage) (aux confitures).**
*ohm-leht' (oh zhahng-bohng') (pahr-mahng-tyay') (oh shahng-pee-
    nyohng') (oh feen-zehrb') (oh froh-mahzh) (oh
    kohng-fee-tewr').*
Omelet (ham) (potato) (mushroom) (small savoury herbs) (cheese)
    (jam).

Pâté de foie gras.
pah-tay duh fwah-grah'.
Goose-liver paste.

Potage au cerfeuil.
poh-tahzh oh sehr-fuhy'.
Soup made of chervil and other herbs; specialty of the Ardennes.

Rágoût de mouton.
rah-goo duh moo-tohng'.
Lamb ragout (stew).

Soupe à l'oignon.
soop ah loh-nyohng'.
Onion soup, mostly served with grated cheese.

Tête de veau vinaigrette.
teht duh voh vee-nay-greht'.
Calf's head with vinegar and oil dressing.

Truite meunière.
trew-eet muh-nee-ehr'.
Brook trout in butter and parsley sauce.

SIGHTSEEING

J'aimerais voir la cathédrale.
zheh-muh-reh vwahr la kah-tay-drahl'.
i would like to see the cathedral.

Et les marchés.
ay lay mar-shay'.
And the market places.

Je voudrais voir des sites historiques.
zhuh voo-dreh' vwahr day seet ees-toh-reek'.
I also want to see some historical sites.

Demain, je veux voir les boîtes de nuit.
duh-mang', zhuh vuh vwahr lay bwaht duh nwee.
Tomorrow, I want to see the night life.

Ne m'envoyez pas à des endroits trop chers.
nuh mahng-vwah-yay pah zah day zahng-drwah' troh shehr.
Don't send me to any expensive places.

Il y a quelques monuments à visiter.
ee lee ah kehlkuh moh-new-mahnt ah vee-zee-tay'.
There are a few monuments to visit.

Pouvons-nous visiter ces ruines?
poo-vohng-noo vee-zee-tay seh rween'?
Can we make a tour of these ruins?

Y a-t-il d'autres endroits intéréssants?
ee a-teel dohtr zahng-drwah zang-teh-reh-sahng'?
Are there any other interesting places?

Je veux voir ce qu'il y a de plus important.
zhuh vuh vwahr suh keel ee a duh plew zang-pohr-tahng'.
I want to see the most important things.

Mais n'allons pas voir trop de choses.
meh nah-lohng-pah vwahr troh duh shohz'.
But let's not see too much.

Je voudrais passer plus de temps ici.
zhuh voo-dreh pah-say plew duh tahng ee-see'.
I want to spend more time here.

Je crois que j'en ai fait assez. Je suis fatigué(e).
zhuh krwah kuh zhahng eh feh a-say'. zhuh swee fah-tee-gay'.
I think I've done enough. I'm tired.

Je voudrais retourner à mon hôtel.
zhuh-voo-dreh' ruh-tour-nay' ah mohn oh-tel'.
I would like to return to my hotel.

SNAPSHOTS FOR REMEMBRANCE

Puis-je prendre une photo de vous?
pweezh prahndr ewn foh-toh duh voo?
Would you mind letting me take your picture?

Continuez votre travail.
kohng-tee-new-ay' vohtr tra-vahy'.
Just continue your work.

Ne regardez pas l'appareil.
nuh ruh-gar-day' pah la-pah-ray'.
Don't look into the camera.

Tournez-vous par ici, s'il vous plaît.
toor-nay-voo par ee-see', seel-voo-pleh'.
Turn this way, please.

Je vous remercie de votre complaisance.
zhuh voo ruh-mehr-see' duh vohtr kohng-pleh-zahng'-s.
Thank you very much for your kindness.

Avez-vous des pellicules en couleur?
ah-vay-voo' deh peh-lee-kewl ahng koo-luhr'?
Do you have color film?

Veuillez développer cette pellicule, s'il vous plaît.
vuh-yay day-vloh-pay' seht peh-lee-kewl, seel-voo-pleh'.
Please develop this roll.

Faites une épreuve de chaque cliché.
feht ewn ay-pruhv duh shahk klee-shay'.
Make one print of each negative.

Quand est-ce que ce sera prêt?
kahng ehs kuh suh suh-rah' preh?
When will it be ready?

Avez-vous du film de cinéma de 16 mm.?
a-vay-voo dew feelm duh see-nay-mah' duh sez mee-lee-mehtr'?
Do you have 16 mm. movie film?

SHOPPING WITH ASSURANCE

Où sont les grands magasins?
oo sohng lay grahng ma-ga-zang'?
Where are the main department stores?

Veuillez m'indiquer une modiste (un chapelier).
vuh-yay mang-dee-kay' ewn moh-deest' (uhng shah-puh-lyeh').
Would you direct me to a small hat shop?

Est-ce trop loin à marcher?
ehs troh lwang ah mahr-shay'?
Is it too far to walk?

Quel autobus m'amènera là?
kehl oh-toh-bews mah-mehn-rah' lah?
What bus will take me there?

Puis-je regarder ce que vous avez?
pew-eezh ruh-gahr-day' suh kuh voo-zah-vay'?
May I look at your merchandise?

Veuillez me montrer un de ceux-là.
vuh-yay muh mohng-tray' uhng duh suh-lah'.
Would you show me one of these?

Où a-t-il été fait?
oo a-teel' ay-tay' feh?
Where was it made?

Combien est-ce que ça coûte?
kohng-bee-ang' ehs-kuh' sah koot?
How much is it?

Faites-moi voir ça.
feht-mwah' vwahr sah.
Let me see that.

Ça me plaît beaucoup, mais c'est trop cher.
sah muh pleh boh-koo', meh seh troh shehr'.
I like this very much, but it is too expensive.

C'est bien. Enveloppez-le, s'il vous plaît.
seh bee-ang'. ahng-vloh-pay'-luh, seel-voo-pleh'.
That is fine. Please wrap it up.

Envoyez-le a mon hôtel, s'il vous plaît.
ahng-vwah-yay-luh' ah mohng oh-tel', seel-voo-pleh'.
Please send it to my hotel.

Mon adresse est 27 rue Blanche.
mohng ah-drehs' ay vang-seht rew blahngsh'.
My address is 27 Rue Blanche.

Je l'emporte.
zhuh lahng-pohrt'.
I will take it with me.

Donnez-moi un reçu, s'il vous plaît.
doh-nay-mwah' uhng ruh-sew', seel-voo-pleh'.
Please let me have a receipt.

J'aimerais voir une robe (un tailler, une jupe).
zheh-muh-reh vwahr ewn rohb (uhng tah-yayr', ewn-zhewp).
I would like to see a dress (suit, skirt).

Je porte la taille américaine numéro 14.
zhuh pohrt lah tahy ah-may-ree-kang new-may-roh kah-tohrz'.
I wear an American size 14.

Je voudrais quelque chose de plus foncé (clair).
zhuh voo-dreh' kehl-kuh shohz duh plew fohng-say' (klehr)
I would like something darker (lighter).

Ceci est trop grand (petit).
suh-see eh troh grahng (puh-tee).
This is too large (small).

De quelle étoffe est-ce fait?
duh kehl ay-tohf' ehs feh?
What material is it made of?

Avez-vous quelque chose de mieux?
ah-vay-voo' kehl-kuh shohz duh myuh?
Have you something better?

Ceci est trop étroit (large).
suh-see 'eh troh pay-trwah' (lahrzh).
This is too tight (loose).

Quelle est la longueur de la robe rouge?
kehl eh lah lohng-guhr duh lah rohb roozh?
How long is the red dress?

Je voudrais une paire de bas, pointure américaine numéro 10.
*zhuh voo-dreh' ewn pehr duh bah, pwahng-tewr ah-may-ree-kehn
       new-may-roh dees'.*
I would like a pair of stockings, American size number 10.

**Où est-ce que je peux acheter une combinaison (un corsage, un sac à
       main, une chemise de nuit, un chapeau, des gants)?**
*oo ehs-kuh zhuh puh ash-tay' ewn kohng-bee-neh-zohng' (blooz, sahr
       ah mang, shuh-meez' duh nwee, shah-poh', deh gahng)?*
Where can I buy a slip (blouse, handbag, nightgown, hat, gloves)?

Dans un grand magasin.
dahng-zuhng grahng mah-gah-zang'.
At a department store.

Prenez l'ascenseur jusqu'au deuxième étage pour les chaussures.
*pruh-nay lah-sahng-suhr zhews-koh duh-zyehm ay-tahzh' poor leh
                                                            shoh-sewr'.*
Take the elevator to the third[1] floor for shoes.

Quel est le prix de ce parfum?
kehl eh luh pree duh suh pahr-fuhng'?
What is the price of this perfume?

Avez-vous un flacon plus petit (plus grand)?
ah-vay-voo uhng flah-kohng' plew puhtee (plew grahng')?
Do you have a smaller (larger) bottle?

Combien coûtent ces boucles d'oreille?
kohng-byang koot seh book-luh doh-reh'-eey?
What is the price of these earrings?

Je n'aime pas ce modèle.
zhuh nehm pah suh moh-dehl'.
I don't like this design.

**Donnez-moi un paquet de cigarettes américaines (un cigare de la
       Havane, des allumettes).**
*doh-nay mwah uhng pah-keh duh see-gah-reht ah-may-ree-kehn'
       (uhng see-gahr' duh lah ah-vahn', deh zah-lew-meht').*
Give me a pack of American cigarets (a Havana cigar, matches).

---

[1] Europeans call "second floor" what in America is called "third floor,"
etc., the ground floor or main floor not being counted as a story.

LAUNDRY AND CLEANING

Faites nettoyer ceci à sec, s'il vous plaît.
feht nay-twah-yay suh-see ah sehk' seel-voo-pleh'.
Please have this dry-cleaned.

Combien de temps est-ce que ça prendra?
kohng-bee-ang' duh tahng es kuh sa prahng-drah'?
How long will it take?

Je voudrais faire repasser ce complet.
zhuh voo-dreh fehr ruh-pah-say' suh kohng-pleh'.
I would like this suit pressed.

Puis-je l'avoir cet après-midi?
pweezh la-vwahr' set a-preh-mee-dee'?
Can I get it back this afternoon?

Ces chemises ont besoin d'être lavées.
seh shuh-meez ohng buh-zwahng' dehtr lah-vay'.
These shirts need laundering.

Ne les amidonnez pas, s'il vous plaît.
nuh lay zah-mee-doh-nay' pah, seel-voo-pleh'.
Please do not starch them.

HAIRDRESSERS AND BARBERS

Pouvez-vous m'indiquer un bon coiffeur?
poo-vay-voo' mang-dee-kay' uhng bohng kwah-fuhr'?
Could you direct me to a good hairdresser?

Madame, veut-elle une permanente?
ma-dahm, vuh-tehl' ewn pehr-ma-nahnt'?
Would madame like a permanent wave?

Combien cela me coûtera-t-il?
kohng-byang' suh-lah muh koo-trah-teel'?
What is the charge?

Cinq mille francs.
sang meel frahng.
Five thousand francs.

Pas aujourd'hui. Mais je voudrais une manucure.
pah zoh-zhoor-dwee'. meh zhuh voo-dreh ewn ma-new-kewr'.
Not today. But I will have a manicure.

Je voudrais un shampooing et une mise en plis.
zhuh-voo-dreh zuhng shahng-pwahng' ay ewn meez ahng plee'.
I would like to have my hair washed and set.

Coupez-moi les cheveux, s'il vous plaît.
koo-pay-mwah leh shuh-vuh', seel-voo-pleh'.
I would like a haircut, please.

Je voudrais me faire raser.
zhuh voo-dreh muh fehr rah-zay'.
I want to have a shave.

GOING TO CHURCH

Je voudrais aller à l'église.
zhuh voo-dreh zah-lay' ah-lay-gleez'.
I would like to go to church.

Où est l'église (la plus proche)?
oo eh lay-gleez' (lah plew prohsh)?
Where is the (nearest) church?

Où est le temple protestant?
oo eh luh tahng'-pl proh-tehs-tahng'?
Where is the Protestant church?

Où est la cathédrale?
oo eh lah ka-tay-drahl'?
Where is the cathedral?

Où est la synagogue?
oo eh lah see-nah-gohg'?
Where is the synagogue?

Où est l'église catholique?
oo eh lay-gleez' kah-toh-leek'?
Where is the Catholic church?

A quelle heure est-ce que commence l'office?
ah kehl uhr ehs kuh koh-mahngs loh-fees'?
At what time does the service begin?

Dans quelle église dit-on la messe en anglais?
dahng kehl ay-gleez dee-tohng lah-mehs ahng ahng-gleh'?
What church holds the mass in English?

Je voudrais un prêtre (pasteur, rabbin) (qui parle anglais).
zhuh voo-dreh uhng prehtr (pah-stuhr, rah-bang) (kee pahrl ahng-gleh').
I would like to see a priest (minister, rabbi) (who speaks English).

Je voudrais me confesser en anglais.
zhuh voo-dreh' muh kohng-feh-say' ahn-ahng-gleh'.
I want to confess in English.

MUSIC HALLS AND THEATERS

Je voudrais deux billets pour les Folies-Bergère.
zhuh voo-dreh duh bee-yay poor lay foh-lee behr-zehr'.
I want two tickets for the Folies Bergère.

En avez-vous pour ce soir?
ahng ah-vay-voo poor suh swahr'?
Have you any for tonight?

Où sont ces places?
oo sohng seh plahs'?
Where are these seats (located)?

Pouvez-vous me montrer un plan de la salle?
poo-vay-voo muh mohng-tray uhng plahng duh la sahl?
Can you show me a seating plan of the theatre?

Je désire des places numérotées.
zhuh day-zeer day plahs new-may-roh-tay'.
I want numbered seats.

NIGHT CLUBS

Je voudrais visiter plusieurs boîtes de nuit.
zhuh voo-dreh vee-zee-tay plew-zyuhr bwaht duh nwee.
I want to visit several night clubs.

J'aimerais voir de bonnes attractions.
zhehm-reh vwahr duh bohn zah-trahk-syohng'.
I am interested in seeing some good floor shows.

Lesquelles recommandez-vous?
leh-kehl' ruh-koh-mahng-day-voo'?
Which ones do you recommend?

Sont-ils très chers?
sohng-teel treh shehr'?
Are they very expensive?

Y a-t-il un couvert?
ee-a-teel uhng koo-vehr'?
Is there a cover charge?

Le champagne, est-il obligatoire?
luh shahng-pahny, eh-teel oh-blee-gah-twahr'?
Is it necessary to buy champagne?

Pas d'extras?
pah dehks-trah'?
No extras?

J'ai commandé du champagne.
zhai koh-mahng-day' dew shahng-pah'nyuh.
I ordered champagne.

EXCHANGING MONEY

Quel est le cours libre du dollar aujourd'hui?
kel ay luh koor leebr dew doh-lahr oh-zhoor-dwee'.
What is today's free market rate on the dollar?

Mais nous ne payons que le cours officiel.
meh noo nuh pay-yohng kuh luh koor oh-fee-syehl'.
But we do not pay anything but the legal rate.

J'ai des travelers chèques.
zheh day tra-vuh-luhr' shek.
I have travelers checks.

Quel est le cours du change?
kel ay luh koor dew shahnzh?
What is the rate of exchange?

Je voudrais encaisser un travelers chèque.
zhuh voo-dreh' ahng-keh-say' uhng tra-vuh-luhr' shek.
I would like to cash a travelers check.

Puis-je avoir mille francs en petites coupures?
pweezh ah-vwahr meel frahng ahng puh-teet' koo-pewr'?
May I have 1,000 francs in small change?

COMMUNICATIONS
Mail

Pardon, où est le bureau de poste le plus proche?
par-dohng', oo ay luh bew-roh duh pohst luh plew prohsh?
Pardon me, where is the nearest post office?

Quel guichet pour la poste aérienne?
kel gee-shay poor la pohst a-ay-ry-en'?
Which window do I go to for airmail?

Quel est le tarif par avion?
kel ay luh tah-reef par a-vee-ohng'?
What is the rate for airmail?

Je désire envoyer ce colis par courrier ordinaire.
zhuh day-zeer ahng-vwah-yay suh koh-lee' par koo-ree-ay or-dee-nehr'.
I wish to send this package by regular mail.

Je voudrais envoyer un pneu.
zhuh voo-dreh ahng-vwah-yay' uhng pnuh'.
I would like to send a letter special delivery.

Je voudrais dix cartes postales.
zhuh voo-dreh dee kahrt pohs-tahl'.
I would like ten post cards.

Où est la boîte aux lettres?
oo eh lah bwaht oh lehtr'?
Where is the mail box?

Telephoning

Avez-vous des jetons pour le téléphone?
ah-vay voo deh zhu-tohng' poor luh tay-lay-fohn'?
Do you have tokens for the telephone?

Donnez-m'en quatre.
doh-nay mahng kahtr'.
Give me four.

Où est l'annuaire?
oo ay la-new-ehr'?
Where is the telephone book?

Où est le téléphone?
oo ay luh tay-lay-fohn'?
Where is the telephone?

Ici Monsieur Dauphin.
ee-see muh-syuh doh-fang'.
This is M. Dauphin calling.

Mademoiselle, je me suis trompé de numéro.
mahd-mwah-zehl, zhuh muh swee trohng-pay duh new-may-roh'.
Operator, I have dialed the wrong number.

Allô. Est-ce bien ici que demeure M. Marceau?
ah-loh. ays byang ee-see kuh duh-muhr muh-syuh mahr-soh'?
Hello. Is this M. Marceau's residence?

A quelle heure l'attendez-vous?
ah kel uhr la-tahng-day-voo'?
When do you expect him?

Pouvez-vous lui faire la commission?
poo-vay-voo' lwee fehr lah koh-mee-syohng'?
Would you give him a message?

Telegrams and Cables

Je voudrais envoyer une dépêche (un télégramme) à Lyon.
zhuh voo-dreh zahng-vwah-yay' ewn day-pehsh (uhng tay-lay-grahm') ah lee-ohng'.
I would like to send a telegram to Lyon.

L'envoyez-vous tarif ordinaire ou tarif différé?
lahng-vwah-yay' voo tah-reef' ohr-dee-nehr oo tah-reef' dee-fay-ray'?
Are you sending it regular or night rate?

Combien coûtent quinze mots?
kohng-byang' koot kangz moh?
How much do fifteen words cost?

Quand arrivera-t-il?
kahng-tah-ree-vrah'-teel?
When will it get there?

TOURIST INFORMATION

Où est le bureau de tourisme le plus proche?
oo ay luh bew-roh' duh too-reezm' luh plew prohsh?
Where is the nearest tourist office?

A quelle heure part le prochain autocar pour Cannes?
ah kehl uhr pahr luh proh-shang' oh-toh-kahr' poor kahn'?
What time is the next bus for Cannes?

Je voudrais visiter un endroit sans touristes.
zhuh voo-dreh vee-zee-tay uhng ahng-drwah sahng too-reest'.
I wish to visit a place where there are no tourists .

Vous avez beaucoup de choix. Par exemple, il y a ce monastère?
*voo zah-vay boh-koo duh shwah'. pahr ehk-zahng-pl' eel-ee-ah suh
    moh-nah-stehr'?*
You have many choices. For example, there is this monastery.

Est-ce que ce village est pittoresque?
ays kuh suh vee-lahzh ay pee-toh-rehsk'?
Is that village picturesque?

Oui, très.
wee, treh.
Yes, very much so.

Est-il difficile d'y aller?
ay-teel dee-fee-seel' dee ah-lay'?
Is it difficult to reach?

Non, il y a un bon service d'autocar.
nohng, eel-ee-ah uhng bohng sehr-vees doh-toh-kahr'.
No, there is frequent bus service.

Y a-t-il un bon hôtel bon marché?
ee-ah-teel uhng bohn oh-tehl bohng mahr-shay'?
Does it have a good, inexpensive hotel?

YOUR HEALTH ABROAD

J'ai mal à l'estomac.
zhay mahl ah lehs-toh-mahk'.
I have an upset stomach.

Je ne me sens pas bien.
zhuh-nuh-muh sahng pah byang'.
I don't feel well.

J'ai besoin d'un docteur (dentiste, oculiste) qui parle anglais.
*zhay buh-zwahng duhng doh-ktuhr' (dahng-teest', oh-kew-leest') kee
    pahrl ahng-gleh'.*
I need a doctor (dentist, oculist) who speaks English.

Je me suis foulé (cassé) la cheville.
zhuh muh swee foo-lay' (kah-say') lah shuh-veey'.
I have sprained (broken) my ankle.

Je me suis coupé.
zhuh muh swee koo-pay'.
I cut myself.

Où est la pharmacie la plus proche?
oo eh lah fahr-mah-see lah plew prohsh?
Where is the nearest drugstore?

Je suis très enrhumé.
zhuh swee treh zahng-rew-may'.
I have a bad cold.

Devrai-je rester au lit?
duh-vray-zh rehs-tay oh lee'?
Will I have to stay in bed?

Je me sens fiévreux.
zhuh muh sahng fyay-vruh'.
I have a fever.

J'ai mal au bras (au dos) (au pied).
zhay mahl oh-brah' (oh-doh') (oh-pyay').
My arm (back) (foot) hurts.

J'ai mal aux dents.
zhay mahl oh-dahng'.
I have a toothache.

Quels sont vos honoraires, docteur?
kehl sohng voh-zoh-noh-rehr', dohk-tuhr'?
What is your fee, doctor?

Pouvez-vous préparer cette ordonnance?
poo-vay-voo pray-pah-ray' seht ohr-doh-nahngs'?
Can you fill this prescription?

Quand sera-t-elle prête?
kahng suh-rah-tehl' preht?
When will it be ready?

Je reviendrai la chercher.
zhuh ruh-vyang-dray' lah shehr-shay'.
I will come back to pick it up.

J'ai cassé mes lunettes. Pouvez-vous remplacer les verres?
zhay kah-say' meh lew-neht'. poo-vay voo rahng-plah-say' leh vehr'?
I have broken my glasses. Can you put in new lenses.

J'ai besoin d'aspirine (de teinture d'iode, d'acide borique).
zhay buh-zwahng dahs-pee-reen (duh tang-tewr dee-ohd', dah-seed').
I need aspirin (iodine, boric acid).

Donnez-moi de l'ouate (du bicarbonate de soude), s'il vous plaît.
doh-nay'-mwah duh lwaht (dew bee-kahr-boh-naht' duh sood),
      seel-voo-pleh'.
Please give me some cotton (bicarbonate of soda).

Des serviettes hygiéniques et un remède contre les douleurs.
deh sehr-vyeht ee-zhyay-neek' ay uhng ruh-mehd' kohng-t'r
Sanitary napkins and a pain reliever.   *leh doo-luhr'.*

Quel remède avez-vous contre l'indigestion?
kehl ruh-mehd ah-vay-voo kohng-t'r lang-dee-zhehs-tyohng'?
Have you anything for indigestion?

Je voudrais des comprimés ou des granulés de préférence.
zhuh voo-dreh deh kohng-pree-may oo deh grah-new-lay duh
      pray-fay-rahng's.
I would like something preferably in tablets or granulated form.

SPORTS

Swimming

Est-ce que je peux louer un maillot (de bain)?
ehs kuh zhuh puh loo-ay uhng mah-yoh' (duh bang')?
Can I rent a suit?

La serviette est-elle comprise dans le prix d'entrée?
la sehr-vyeht ay-tehl kohng-preez' dahng luh pree dahng-tray'?
Is the towel included in the price of admission?

Je voudrais louer une cabine.
zhuh voo-dreh loo-ay ewn kah-been'.
I would like to rent a cabin.

Combien est-ce?
kohng-byang' ehs?
What is the charge?

La piscine est-elle javélisée?
la pee-seen' ay-tehl' zhah-veh-lee-zay'?
Is the pool chlorinated?

Vendez-vous de l'ambre solaire?
vahng-day-voo duh lahng-br soh-lehr'?
Do you sell suntan oil?

Golf

Puis-je avoir un set de clubs?
pweezh a-vwahr uhng set duh kluhb'?
Can I have a set of clubs?

Allez-vous me donner un bon caddy?
a-lay-voo muh doh-nay uhng bohng kah-dee'?
Will you provide me with a good caddy?

Je voudrais acheter des balles de golf.
zhuh voo-dreh zahsh-tay day bahl duh gohlf'.
I wish to buy some golf balls.

Tennis

Quel est le tarif de location d'un court?
kehl eh luh tah-reef duh loh-kah-syohng duhng koor?
What is the charge for the use of a court?

Puis-je louer une raquette?
pweezh loo-ay' ewn rah-ket'?
Can I have a racket?

Où est le vestiaire des hommes?
oo ay luh vehs-tyehr deh-zohm'?
Where is the men's locker room?

CONDUCTING BUSINESS

Je voudrais un permis de séjour.
zhuh voo-dreh uhng pehr-mee duh say-zhoor'.
I wish to apply for a sojourn card.

Si je quitte ce district, que dois-je faire?
see zhuh keet suh dees-treekt', kuh dwahzh fehr?
If I move from this district, what must I do?

Voici ma carte d'identité française.
vwah-see ma kahrt dee-dahng-tee-tay frahng-sehz'.
Here is my French identity card.

Je n'ai pas de casier judiciaire.
zhuh nay'-pah duh kah-syay' zhew-dee-syehr'.
I have no criminal record.

Je voudrais entrer en relations avec une maison de textiles.
zhuh voo-dreh zahng-tray ahng ruh-lah-syohng ah-vehk ewn meh-zohng duh tehks-teel'.
I would like to contact a textile firm.

Je représente une maison américaine.
zhuh ruh-pray-zahnt ewn meh-zohng a-may-ree-ken'.
I represent an American firm.

Comment puis-je vérifier le crédit d'une maison?
koh-mahng pweezh vay-ree-fee-ay luh kray-dee dewn meh-zohng?
How can I check on a firm's credit rating?

Combien de personnes employez-vous?
kohng-bee-ang duh pehr-sohn ahng-plwah-yay-voo'?
How many people do you employ?

Puis-je inspecter votre usine?
pweezh ans-pehk-tay vohtr ew-zeen'?
May I inspect your plant?

Je voudrais des références bancaires.
zhuh voo-dreh day ray-fay-rahns bahn-kehr'.
I would like bank references.

Je payerai les marchandises en dollars.
zhuh pay-uh-ray' leh mar-shahng-deez ahng doh-lahr'.
I will pay in dollars for the goods.

Quand pouvez-vous envoyer la marchandise?
kahng poo-vay-voo ahng-vwah-yay lah mar-shahng-deez'?
When can you ship the merchandise?

OUTLINE OF FRENCH GRAMMAR

Although, for purposes of everyday practical needs, you will be able to get by with some stock of common French words and phrases, it is advisable also to have some understanding of the parts of speech and their various forms as well as of the manner in which French sentences are constructed. In the following pages we have attempted to present the "highlights" of French grammar very concisely, so as to enable you to understand the how and why of the phrases in this book. This survey is of necessity brief, but the main facts for your daily needs have been covered.

1. THE ARTICLE

1.1. In French, nouns are either of the masculine or the feminine gender. The definite article *le* precedes masculine nouns, whereas *la* is used for feminine nouns: *le livre* (the book), *la maison* (the house). Before a vowel and before a mute *h*, both *le* and *la* are shortened to *l'*: *l'ami* (from "le ami": the friend, masculine), *l'amie* (from "la amie": the girl-friend or lady-friend), *l'hôtel* (from "le hôtel": the hotel), *l'histoire* (from "la histoire": the story). The plural of the definite article is invariably *les* for both genders: *les amis, les amies, les livres, les maisons, les hôtels.*

1.2. The indefinite article is invariably *un* for the masculine and *une* for the feminine: *un livre, un ami, un hôtel; une maison, une amie, une histoire* (a book, a friend, etc.).

1.3. French differs from English in the use of the articles: *il est rédacteur* (he is an editor). (See pages 14 and 15 for more examples.)

1.4. Contractions of the definite article. Combinations of the words *à* (at, to, for) and *de* (of, for) with *le* and *les* are written and pronounced as follows: *au* instead of "à le"; *aux* instead of "à les"; *du* instead of "de le"; *des* instead of "de les." This rule is invariable and should be observed carefully.

1.5. The partitive article. It is a peculiarity of the French language that when an indefinite quantity of something is discussed, this quantity is thought of as *part* of the whole. When we say "Here is butter," the Frenchman will say "Here is of the butter," i.e. "some of all the butter there is." This imparts a *partitive* meaning to the sentence. The partitive article is therefore not used when a definite quantity is indicated. "Here is the butter" is translated as "Voici *le* beurre," and "Here is (some) butter" as "Voici *du* beurre."

The partitive article, which is used with the meaning of "some", "any", consists of the preposition *de* followed by the definite article: *du tabac, de la confiture, des hommes, des femmes.* However, after an adverb of negation or *beaucoup* (much), *un peu* (a little) and most expressions of quantity, *de* is used alone: *Je n'ai pas de pain* (I have no bread); *il n'a pas acheté beaucoup de légumes* (He didn't buy many vegeables).

2. THE NOUN: GENDER AND NUMBER

2.1. Generally speaking, names and designations of male persons and animals are masculine: *l'homme* (the man), *le peintre* (the painter), *le chien* (the dog). Similarly, the nouns designating female persons and animals are mostly feminine: *la mère* (the mother), *une chatte* (a cat), *la bonne* (the maid). The feminine form of masculine nouns can often be formed by adding -e or by doubling the final consonant of the noun and adding an *e* to the original noun: *ami-amie; patron-patronne* (owner, chief, boss). There are some special endings which indicate the masculine and the feminine form of a large number of words. The most important of these suffixes are: *-er, -eur, -eau, -ien, -ier, -f, -on* for the masculine; and *-esse, -euse, -elle, -ière, -ette, -ie, -ienne, -onne, -ve, -trice* for the feminine.

2.2. The plural of most nouns is formed by adding -s to the singular. However, words ending in -s, -x, -z remain unchanged. Words ending in -al change into -aux (*cheval-chevaux*) except for a few of them which follow the general rule (*bal-bals*). Some nouns in -ail also form their plural in -aux (*travail-travaux*), but most of them add only an *s* (*rail-rails*). Several common nouns in -ou form their plural in -x (*bijou-bijoux*). The words *ciel* (sky) and *oeil* (eye) have completely irregular plurals which are respectively *cieux* and *yeux*.

Proper names remain unchanged in the plural: *Les Martin* (The Martins).

3. THE ADJECTIVE

3.1.a. Qualifying adjectives. These indicate a quality of the noun to which they refer. They correspond in gender and number with that noun: *un bon père* (a good father), *de beaux livres* (beautiful books), *une jeune fille aimable* (a nice girl), *des maisons charmantes* (lovely houses). They generally follow the noun, except for a number of adjectives which normally precede the noun, the most important of which are: *bon* (good), *beau* (beautiful), *jeune* (young), *vieux* (old), *grand* (large), *petit* (small), *court* (short), *long* (long), *mauvais* (bad), *nouveau* (new). For special emphasis, it is permissible, however, to place these adjectives after the noun, and conversely those adjectives which generally follow the noun may be placed before it for the same reason.

3.1.b. The plural of adjectives is generally formed by adding *-s* to the singular. The feminine is formed by adding *-e* to the masculine form, and the feminine plural by adding *-es: joli-jolis; jolie-jolies*. In general, the same rules apply as for the formation of feminine and plural of nouns. Special rules: Words ending in *-f* take *-ve* for the feminine. Words ending in *-x* take *-se* (*heureux-heureuse*) with the following exceptions: *doux-douce, faux-fausse, vieux-vieille*. Words in *er* take *-ère: une histoire policière* (a detective story). Words ending in *-c* take *-che* (*franc, franche*). Many double their last consonant before adding the *e* (*gros-grosse, sot-sotte*). The adjectives *beau* and *vieux* each have another masc. singular form, *bel* and *vieil* which are used before a noun beginning with a vowel or a mute *h* (*un bel arbre, un vieil homme*).

3.1.c. Note that **nouns do not generally function as** adjectives in French; in order to translate "desk lamp" you should transform the phrase into "lamp of desk": *lampe de bureau*. Remember, however, that *une tasse de café* means "a cup of coffee," but *une tasse à café* means "a coffee cup" (*à* meaning "for").

3.1.d. In forming the *comparative*, the adjective does not change its form (as often happens in English), but is preceded by *plus* (more) and followed by *que* (than): *un maître jovial* (a jolly teacher), *un maître plus jovial* (a jollier teacher); *elle est plus rapide que lui* (she is faster than he). The *superlative* is translated with *le plus* (the most): *le plus joli* (the prettiest). Exceptions: "Good-better-best" is translated with *bon—meilleur—le meilleur;* "bad-worse-the worst" as *mauvais—pire—le pire* (but also regularly as *mauvais—plus mauvais—le plus mauvais);* "small-smaller-the smallest" as *petit—plus petit—le plus petit,* but "small (meaning little or few)-less-the least" as *peu (de)—moindre—le moindre.* The adverb of *moindre* is *moins;* "less good than" is translated as *moins bon (bons, bonne, bonnes) que.* "As . . . as" is translated by *aussi . . . que;* "not so . . . as" by *pas si . . . que.* "As much (many) . . . as" and "not so much (many) . . . as" are rendered by *autant . . . que* and *pas tant . . . que,* respectively.

3.2. The **possessive adjectives** agree in gender and number with
the noun to which they refer. Their forms are as follows:

English	Masc. sing.	Fem. sing.	Masc. & fem. plural
my	mon	ma*	mes
your (familiar)	ton	ta*	tes
his, her, its	son	sa*	ses
our	notre	notre	nos
your (polite)	votre	votre	vos
their	leur	leur	leurs

This shows that the possessive adjectives do not indicate the sex
of the possessor, but the grammatical gender of the thing possessed.
son livre can mean "his book" as well as "her book"; in case of
ambiguity, use the construction with the personal pronoun: *son livre
à lui* and *son livre à elle,* respectively.

3.3. The demonstrative adjectives. "This" and "that" are translated by *ce* for masculine nouns, *cet* for masculine nouns beginning
with a vowel or mute *h, cette* for feminine nouns, and *ces* for both
genders in the plural. If it is desired, a further distinction may be
made between "this" and "that" by adding the adverbial particles
-ci and *-là* to the nouns: *cette jeune fille-ci* (this girl); *ces garçons-là*
(those boys). (*Ci* is an abbreviated form of the adverb *ici,* meaning
"here," and *là* is the word for "there.")

3.4. The interrogative adjective. This can be expressed in only
one way, namely with the word *quel,* meaning "what" or "which."
The basic form *quel* becomes *quelle* for the feminine, and *quels* and
quelles for the masculine and feminine plural, respectively. *Quel* can
also be used in exclamations and then means "what a," such as in
quelle brute! (what a rude fellow!). (This example also shows that the
grammatical gender is not necessarily the same as the logical gender.)

3.5. The **indefinite adjectives** indicate an unspecified amount or
quantity of the subject or object expressed by the noun. The most
important forms are:

Aucun (-e, -s, -es): il n'a aucun argent (he doesn't have any money).
Nul (-lle, -s, -les): "none at all": *nulle part* (nowhere).
Chaque (inv.): each, every. *Chaque maison* (each house). But: *Les
femmes gagnent deux mille francs chacune* (the women earn 2000
fr. each).

---

*Before a vowel or mute *h,* the forms *ma, ta* and *sa* become *mon, ton,
son,* as in *mon âme* (my soul), *son honnêteté* (his or her integrity).

Plusieurs (invariable): several. *Plusieurs erreurs* (several errors).

Tout (-e, tous, toutes): all, entire. *Tout le monde* (everybody).

Quelque (-s): Some, a few. *Quelques villes* (a few towns). *Quelqu* *fois:* sometimes.

Certain (-e, -s, -es): certain. *Certains individus* (certain persons).

Tel (-le, -s, -les): such, similar. *Une telle conduite est peu convenab* (such behavior is not very appropriate).

3.6. The numerals. The *cardinal* numbers are as follows:

1. un (une)	12. douze	30. trente
2. deux	13. treize	40. quarante
3. trois	14. quatorze	50. cinquante
4. quatre	15. quinze	60. soixante
5. cinq	16. seize	70. soixante-dix
6. six	17. dix-sept	71. soixante et onze
7. sept	18. dix-huit	80. quatre-vingts
8. huit	19. dix-neuf	81. quatre-vingt-un
9. neuf	20. vingt	90. quatre-vingt-dix
10. dix	21. vingt et un	91. quatre-vingt-onze
11. onze	22. vingt-deux	100. cent

Remarks: *Vingt* and *cent* are invariable if followed by anoth numeral: 80 francs is *quatre-vingts francs,* but 98 francs is *quatr vingt-dix-huit francs;* 700 books is *sept cents livres,* but 763 books *sept cent soixante-trois livres.* The word for 1000 is *mille,* which invariable. A million is *un million.*

The following are the basic *ordinal* numbers, from which the for of other desired numbers can easily be derived:

1st. premier (première)	16th. seizième
2nd. deuxième	17th. dix-septième
3rd. troisième	18th. dix-huitième
4th. quatrième	19th. dix-neuvième
5th. cinquième	20th. vingtième
6th. sixième	21st. vingt et unième
7th. septième	22nd. vingt-deuxième
8th. huitième	30th. trentième
9th. neuvième	78th. soixante-dix-huitième
10th. dixième	100th. centième
11th. onzième	900th. neuf-centième
12th. douzième	1000th. millième
13th. treizième	millionth. millionième
14th. quatorzième	1958th. mil-neuf-cent-
15th. quinzième	cinquante-huitième

Simpler forms of numerals. If you plan to utilize your knowledge f French in Belgium or in certain regions of Switzerland and northrn and southern France, you will be glad to know that the somewhat omplicated forms *soixante-dix* (70), *quatre-vingts* (80) and *quatrengt-dix* (90) are replaced by the much easier forms **septante, octante** nd **nonante,** with **septantième, octantième** and **nonantième** for the rdinal numerals. These forms, although not used in the standard anguage of France, will be readily understood everywhere.

4. THE PRONOUNS

4.0. We distinguish personal, reflexive, possessive, demonstrative, elative and interrogative pronouns.

4.1. The **personal pronouns,** according to their position and meanng in the sentence, function as subject, indirect-object, direct-object nd prepositional pronouns. Their forms are as follows:

English equivalent	Subject	Indirect object	Direct object	Prepositional
I, to me, me, (with) me, etc.	je	me	me	moi*
you (familiar, singular)	tu	te	te	toi*
he, it, him, etc.	il	lui	le	lui*
she, etc.	elle	lui	la	elle
we, etc.	nous	nous	nous	nous
you (familiar & polite plural and polite sing.)	vous	vous	vous	vous
they, etc. (m.)	ils	leur	les	eux*
they, etc. (fem.)	elles	leur	les	elles

Moi and *toi* are also used after an affirmative imperative, *Donnez-oi.* (Give me.).

Examples: *Je te dis de venir* (I tell you to come), *moi, je pense à i* (I am thinking of you), *donnez-lui l'argent* (give him the money), *onnez-le-lui* (give it to him or her).

4.2. The position of the personal pronouns in the sentence may e derived from the following summarized rules:

1. The subject pronouns are used with the verb, but their emphatic rms can stand alone: *Je parle. Qui parle? Moi.* (I speak. Who eaks? I.)

---

*These forms are also used as the subject in order to obtain more mphasis: *C'est lui qui parle* (It is he who speaks).

2. Both the direct and indirect objects precede the verb, but not ▮ the affirmative imperative. When both the direct and indirect obje▮ occur in one sentence, the indirect object precedes the direct obje▮ but not when both are in the third person, and not in the affirmati▮ imperative. Examples: *il me le donne* (he gives it to me); *il le l▮ donne* (he gives it to him or her); *donnez-le-moi* (give it to me), *ne ▮ le donnez pas* (don't give it to me); *il la leur donne* (he gives it ▮ them; *la* here takes the place of a feminine article and *leur* can re▮ to both men and women.

4.3. Two very important words in French are *y* (meaning "there▮ "at that place" or "to[ward] that place") and *en* (meaning "of i▮ "of them," "a quantity of" or "from there"). Their position is g▮ erned by the second rule, above, and they are *always* preceded by t▮ pronouns. Examples: *Avez-vous des poires? Oui, j'en ai. Non, je n'▮ ai pas.* (Do you have pears? Yes, I have [some of them]. No, I have▮ any.) *Allez-vous au village? Oui, j'y vais. Non, je n'y vais pas.* (A▮ you going to the village? Yes, I am [going to it]. No, I am not going ▮ it.) *Revient-il de France? Oui, il en revient* (Is he coming back fr▮ France? Yes, he is coming back from there.) Important idiom: *J'y su▮* (now I understand you! I get you!; lit.: I am there!).

4.4. The impersonal pronoun *on*, which can only be used as ▮ subject, has no English equivalent and may be translated as a▮ person of the subject pronouns depending on its meaning in t▮ sentence. The French often use it when in English a passive for▮ would be used. Examples: *Y a-t-il une grève? Non, on travaille.* ▮ there a strike? No, we, or they, are working.) *Dépêchez-vous, on pa▮* (Hurry up, we are leaving, or the train, or the bus, is leaving.) *Co▮ ment allez-vous? Ça va, on s'arrange.* (How are you doing? Reasonab▮ well, I manage.) *On pense qu'il fera beau temps.* (It is thought tha▮ will be, or we will have, good weather.) *Pour la gare, on prend la p▮ mière rue à gauche.* (To the station, you take the first street to yo▮ left.) See also impersonal verbs, **8.8.**

4.5. The **reflexive pronouns** are *me, te, se, nous, vous, se*. *Se* c▮ also mean "each other." Examples: *Je me lave* (I wash myself); *▮ s'aiment* (they love themselves, or they love each other).

4.6. The **possessive pronouns** (to be distinguished from the poss▮ sive adjectives, discussed earlier) are preceded by an article.

English	Masc. sing.	Fem. sing.	Masc. plur.	Fem. plur.
mine	le mien	la mienne	les miens	les miennes
yours	le tien	la tienne	les tiens	les tiennes
his, hers, its	le sien	la sienne	les siens	les siennes

English	Masc. sing.	Fem. sing.	Masc. plur.	Fem. plur.
ours	le nôtre	la nôtre	les nôtres	les nôtres
yours	le vôtre	la vôtre	les vôtres	les vôtres
theirs	le leur	la leur	les leurs	les leurs

Examples: *Ma maison et la sienne* (my house and his or hers), *leurs enfants et les vôtres* (their children and yours).

4.7. The **demonstrative pronouns** take the place of a noun that has just been used in order to avoid repetition: In "John's bicycle and Peter's" we use "that of Peter" instead of "Peter's": *la bicyclette de Jean et celle de Pierre.*

The forms are *celui, celle, ceux, celles.* Independently used, the forms are *celui-ci,* etc., and *celui-là,* etc., respectively. Example: *Voyez-vous ces deux voitures? Celle-ci est la mienne, et celle-là appartient à mon frère.* (Do you see these two cars? This one is mine, and that one belongs to my brother.)

4.8. The **relative pronouns** are *qui* when relating to the subject, and *que* when relating to an object: *l'homme qui parle* (the man who speaks), *l'homme que je vois* (the man whom I see); *le livre qui est sur la table* (the book which is on the table), *le livre que je lis* (the book which I read). "Of whom" and "of which" are rendered by *dont: l'écrivain dont je vous ai parlé* (the writer of whom I spoke to you), *la pièce dont j'ai lu la critique* (the play the review of which I read). After a preposition, the forms *que* and *dont* cannot be used. In such cases use *lequel* (masc. sing.), *laquelle* (fem. sing.), *lesquels* (masc. plur.) and *lesquelles* (fem. plur.), in combination with the desired preposition. In the case of, e.g., *avec* (with) we get a phrase like *le marteau avec lequel je travaille* (the hammer with which I work). But the prepositions *à* and *de* melt together with the article *le* into *au* and *du*, respectively, so that the compound forms become *auquel, duquel, auxquels, auxquelles, desquels, desquelles,* etc., as explained in the chapter on the Article.

4.9. The **interrogative pronouns** are *qui* (who, whom) for persons and *que* (what) for animals and things. Instead of *que*, the French like to use the longer forms *qu'est-ce qui* (what? what is it that?) for the subject, and *qu'est-ce que* for the object. *Qui* also has the longer forms: *qui est-ce qui* (subject) and *qui est-ce que* (direct object). *Quoi* (what) is used for the neuter in connection with an indefinite pronoun and for objects after a preposition: *on ne sait pas quoi faire* (we don't know what to do); *de quoi parlez-vous?* (what are you talking about?). Important idiom: *il n'y a pas de quoi* (don't mention it; it is nothing). "Which," in making a choice, is translated by *lequel, laquelle, lesquels,* *lesquelles: Lequel des trois hôtels préférez-vous* (which of the three hotels do you prefer?), *lesquelles de ces jeunes filles ont leur bacca-lauréat?* (which [plural] of these girls have graduated from high school?). Other examples: *qui vient?* or *qui est-ce qui vient?* (who is coming?), *que dites-vous?* or *qu'est-ce que vous dites?* (what do you say?), *qu'est-ce qui vous arrive?* (what's happening to you?), *à qui est-ce que vous direz la vérité?* (to whom will you tell the truth?). In a phrase like *les pages du livre lesquelles vous avez copiées* we use *lesquelles* to indicate the *pages* of the book you have copied. *Que* would be ambiguous, because it might refer to either the pages or to the book itself. If it were the *book* that had been copied, the phrase would be *les pages du livre lequel vous avez copié*. Note that French, in this respect, is more logical and clear than English. (The forms of the past participle *copié* and *copiées* are explained in the introductory remarks on the verb; see **8.4**).

5. THE ADVERBS

5.1. The adverbs are generally formed by adding the adverbial ending *-ment* to the feminine form of the adjective, e.g. *définitif* (definite), *définitive* (fem. adj.), *définitivement* (adv.). However, those adjectives which end in *-ant* form their adverbs with *-amment,* such as *courant, couramment,* and adjectives ending in *-ent* take *-emment* for their adverbs: *intelligent—intelligemment.*

5.2. The comparative and superlative of the adverbs are formed analogously to those of the adjectives, q.v., with *plus* and *le plus,* respectively. The following forms are irregular: *bien* (well), *mieux* (better); *mal* (badly), *pis* (worse); *peu* (little), *moins* (less).

5.3. Important adverbs are:

Of place: *ailleurs* (elsewhere), *autour* (around), *dedans* (within) *dehors* (outside), *derrière* (behind), *dessus* (upon), *dessous* (below), *devant* (before), *ici* (here), *là* (there), *loin* (far), *où* (where), *partout* (everywhere), *près* (near), *y* (there);

Of time: *alors* (then), *aujourd'hui* (today), *aussitôt* (at once), *autrefois* (formerly), *avant* (before), *bientôt* (soon), *déjà* (already), *demain* (tomorrow), *depuis* (since), *enfin* (finally), *hier* (yesterday), *jamais* (never), *parfois* (sometimes), *quelquefois* (sometimes), *souvent* (often), *toujours* (always).

5.4. "Not" is translated by *ne . . . pas: je travaille* (I work), *je ne travaille pas* (I don't work). An emphatic negative may be expressed by *pas du tout: je ne travaille pas du tout* (I definitely am not working)

Never" is translated by *ne . . . jamais: je ne travaille jamais* (I never work). The negative implication of "nobody" and "nothing" is also expressed adverbially: *personne ne m'a vu, je n'ai vu personne* (nobody has seen me, I haven't seen anybody) ; *rien n'est à bon marché* (nothing is inexpensive), *je n'ai rien acheté* (I bought nothing).

6. THE CONJUNCTIONS

6.0. The conjunctions are invariable words or phrases which link two principal clauses or a principal clause and a dependent clause; they also join all other grammatical categories of equal rank, such as nouns and nouns, adjectives and adjectives, etc., by words as "and," "or," "either . . . or," "neither . . . nor," etc.

6.1. Some important coordinating conjunctions (which link elements of equal nature) and subordinating conjunctions (which introduce a dependent clause) are:

ainsi (thus)
aussi (hence; also)
car (for, because)
cependant (however)
comme (as, since, because)
donc (therefore, thus)
et (and)
mais (but)
néanmoins (nevertheless)

ni (nor)
or (now)
puisque (since)
quand (when)
que (that)
quoique (although)
si (if)
soit (be it)
toutefois (but, however)

6.2. Conjunctive phrases have the function of conjunctions. A few useful forms are:

à condition que (provided that)*
ainsi que (so that)
afin que (in order that)*
alors que (when, whereas)
à mesure que (to the degree that)
à moins que (unless)*
après que (after)
aussitôt que (as soon as)
avant que (before)*
bien que (although)*

de même que (as well as)
de peur que (for fear that)*
depuis que (since)
de sorte que (so that)*
dès que (since the time that)
jusqu'à ce que (until)*
parce que (because)
pour que (in order that)*
sans que (without)*
tandis que (while, whereas)

The ones with an * are followed by the subjunctive; see **8.5.**

7. THE INTERJECTIONS

7.1. Interjections are words that express a feeling (joy, pain, surprise, etc.), and may consist of one invariable word or may also be a phrase of two or even more words used as exclamations. Some often-used forms with their approximate English equivalents are:

Ah! (ha!)
attention! (watch out!)
allons! (let's go!)
bah! (who cares!)
bon! (good!)
comment! (how!)
courage! (courage!)
d'accord! (o.k.!)
dites donc! (say!)
eh bien! (well now!)

en avant! (forward!)
entendu! (all right!)
gare! (take care!)
halte! (stop!)
hélas! (alas!)
holà! (go easy!)
malheur! (too bad!)
parbleu! (heck!; darn it!)
silence! (quiet!)
tiens! (look!; how odd!)

8. THE VERBS

8.1. French verbs correspond in number and person with their subjects. If the subject is in the first person singular, the verb is also in the first person singular, etc.

8.2. The **compound tenses,** just as in English, are constructed with *avoir* (to have) plus the past participle. However, *all* reflexive verbs (see the section on reflexive pronouns) are constructed with *être* (to be) as in *je me suis lavé* (I washed myself); but *j'ai lavé les fenêtres* (I washed the windows).

Contrary to the general rule, nearly all verbs expressing *movement* form their compound tenses with the auxiliary verb *être*. Some of those verbs, which you will do well to remember, are *aller* (to go), *arriver* (to arrive), *devenir* (to become), *partir* (to leave), *retourner* (to return), *sortir* (to go out), *tomber* (to fall) and *venir* (to come). *Rester* (to remain, to stay) is also conjugated with *être*.

8.3. Whereas English has various ways to express the *present* tense ("I speak," "I am speaking," "I do speak"), French has only one such way: *je parle.* The *past* can be expressed by the simple or the compound tense. The *imperfect* is the descriptive tense, which may describe a prolonged action or condition in the past, in the course of which another action or fact took place. The present perfect expresses one single event that took place in the past. In *je travaillais quand il est arrivé* (I was working when he arrived), *travaillais* is the imperfect or descriptive tense, and *est arrivé* is the present perfect. Note that the *passé simple* (preterit) is no longer used in modern spoken French and will therefore not be discussed here. It has gradually been replaced by the present perfect.

The *future* is not expressed, as in English, by means of a special verb (shall or will) but is a separate verbal form: *je parlerai* (I shall speak).

8.4. The past participle always agrees in gender and number with the noun of which it is either the attribute or the adjective. Examples: *l'argent était perdu* (the money was lost), *la guerre était perdue* (the war was lost); *l'argent perdu* (the lost money), *la guerre perdue* (the lost war). If the subject consists of a masculine and a feminine noun, the past participle (or adjective) is in the masculine plural form: *le monsieur et la dame sont partis* (the gentleman and the lady have left).

In the case of verbs conjugated with *avoir,* the past participle agrees in gender and number with the object *only* if the object precedes the verb; the past participle does not change (i.e., the basic masculine singular form is used) if the object comes after it: *les tables que j'ai achetées* (the tables which I bought); *j'ai acheté les tables* (I bought the tables); *il l'a trouvé* (he found him); *il l'a trouvée* (he found her).

8.5.a. Whereas in English we use verbs almost exclusively in the indicative mood, even when we express a wish or doubt, it is necessary in French to distinguish carefully between indicative and subjunctive. Established facts, statements, definite expectations, and any state, act or happening representing actual fact require the indicative; but if a state, condition, event or act is desirable, necessary, possible, conditional, doubtful, dependent or questionable, the subjunctive *must* be used: *Je sais qu'il sera en retard.* (I know that he is going to be late); *Je crains qu'il ne soit en retard.* (I am afraid that he'll be late); *Nous admirons le choix qu'il a fait.* (We admire the choice that he has made); *Nous partageons les idées qu'il a exprimées.* (We share the ideas that he has expressed); *Nous doutons que ses idées soient justes.* (We doubt that his ideas are just).

8.5.b. The subjunctive is also used after impersonal expressions such as: *il faut que* (it is essential that); *il est important que* (it is important that); *il est impossible que* (it is impossible that), etc. The word *que* (that) is always used in French even though it is not always translated in English: *Il est essentiel qu'il le sache.* (It is essential that he should do it); *Il est surprenant qu'il le croie.* (It is surprising that he should believe it); *Il faut que je parte.* (I must go). The subjunctive always follows certain conjunctions (see **6.2**): *Je sortirai à moins qu'il ne pleuve.* (I'll go out unless it rains); *Il a tort bien qu'il ne veuille* *pas l'admettre.* (He is wrong even though he does not want to admit it); *Téléphonez-nous afin que nous vous attendions.* (Call us so that we may wait for you).

8.5.c. The subjunctive is used nearly exclusively in dependent (subordinate) clauses. In some exclamatory sentences it is used independently: *vive la France!* (long live France!). This is really an abbreviated way of saying *je souhaite que la France vive* (I wish that France may live).

8.5.d. An important exception to the general rule given in 8.5.a is formed by the word *si* (if), which is **always** followed by the indicative, even when expressing a wish, necessity, condition, doubt, etc.: *je voyagerais si j'avais de l'argent* (I would travel if I had money); *vous devrez travailler si vous voulez réussir* (you will have to work if you want to succeed); *si seulement ma femme revenait!* (if only my wife would come back!).

8.6. The regular verbs can be divided into four groups of conjugations according to the endings of the infinitive, *-er, -ir, -oir,* and *-re.* The following conjugation patterns for one regular verb of each of the four groups will enable you to know the correct forms of the other regular verbs. Some verbs deviate in minor details from the regular pattern for reasons of euphony. (For instance, the first person singular of the otherwise regular verb *acheter* is **achète** rather than *achete,* but the first person plural is formed regularly because the pronunciation does not require an accent: *achetons.*)

Infinitive

Parler *(to speak)*	**Finir** *(to end)*	**Recevoir** *(to receive)*	**Rompre** *(to break)*

Present Participle

parlant	finissant	recevant	rompant

Past Participle

parlé	fini	reçu	rompu

Imperative

parle *(familiar sing.)*	finis	reçois	romps
parlons *(1st per. pl.)*	finissons	recevons	rompons
parlez *(polite sing. and fam. & pol. pl.)*	finissez	recevez	rompez

INDICATIVE

Present

e parle	finis	reçois	romps
u parles	finis	reçois	romps
parle	finit	reçoit	rompt
ous parlons	finissons	recevons	rompons
ous parlez	finissez	recevez	rompez
ls parlent	finissent	reçoivent	rompent

Imperfect

e parlais	finissais	recevais	rompais
u parlais	finissais	recevais	rompais
parlait	finissait	recevait	rompait
ous parlions	finissions	recevions	rompions
ous parliez	finissiez	receviez	rompiez
s parlaient	finissaient	recevaient	rompaient

Future

e parlerai	finirai	recevrai	romprai
u parleras	finiras	recevras	rompras
parlera	finira	recevra	rompra
ous parlerons	finirons	recevrons	romprons
ous parlerez	finirez	recevrez	romprez
ls parleront	finiront	recevront	rompront

Present Perfect

ai parlé	j'ai fini	j'ai reçu	j'ai rompu
u as parlé	tu as fini	tu as reçu	tu as rompu
a parlé	il a fini	il a reçu	il a rompu
ous avons parlé	nous avons fini	nous avons reçu	nous avons rompu
ous avez parlé	vous avez fini	vous avez reçu	vous avez rompu
ls ont parlé	ils ont fini	ils ont reçu	ils ont rompu

CONDITIONAL

e parlerais	finirais	recevrais	romprais
u parlerais	finirais	recevrais	romprais
parlerait	finirait	recevrait	romprait
ous parlerions	finirions	recevrions	romprions
ous parleriez	finiriez	recevriez	rompriez
ls parleraient	finiraient	recevraient	rompraient

SUBJUNCTIVE   Present

que je parle	finisse	reçoive	rompe
que tu parles	finisses	reçoives	rompes
qu'il parle	finisse	reçoive	rompe
que nous parlions	finissions	recevions	rompions
que vous parliez	finissiez	receviez	rompiez
qu'ils parlent	finissent	reçoivent	rompent

How to form Interrogative Sentences

8.7. A question can be expressed: 1) by prefixing *est-ce que* (is it that) to a declarative statement: *Est-ce que vous parlez français?;* 2) by inverting the verb and its subject pronoun and joining them with a hyphen: *parlez-vous français?;* 3) by making a statement and adding *n'est-ce pas?* (isn't it so?) for confirmation: *vous parlez français, n'est-ce pas?;* 4) in conversation, by using a rising inflection at the end of a declarative statement: *vous parlez français?* The rising inflection and the *est-ce que* form are frequent in conversation.

The following points must be remembered about the use of the inversion: a) *est-ce que* is used instead of inversion in the first person singular of the present tense (except in verbs such as *puis-je? dois-je? ai-je? suis-je?*); b) for reasons of euphony, the letter *t* is inserted between verb and pronoun in the third person singular of the present tense of first conjugation verbs: *parle-t-il? parle-t-elle?*, as well as in the third person future tense of **all** verbs: *parlera-t-il? finira-t-elle? rompra-t-il? sera-t-elle? viendra-t-il?*); c) if there is a noun subject, the noun stands first while an extra (redundant) pronoun is used in the inversion with the verb: *Le touriste parle-t-il français?*, as the noun subject cannot follow the verb.

Impersonal Verbs

8.8. Impersonal verbs can have no other subject than the indefinite pronoun *il (it)*. Examples: *il pleut* (it rains), *il neige* (it snows), *il faut* (it is necessary [from *falloir;* see list of irregular verbs and also **8.5** on the subjunctive, by which this verb is always followed]).

THE IRREGULAR VERBS

8.9. Just as in English, French irregular verbs can be irregular in most of their tenses and persons, but in others the irregularities are limited to a few details of spelling. Listed below are some frequently used irregular verbs. Note that only the irregular forms are presented, and that in general the forms which are not given can be derived regularly, taking into account that *the stem of the verb generally is preserved most purely in the **present participle,** from which most of the derived tenses are formed*. Note, further, that the conditional

lways follows the pattern of the future, so that the conditional is
egular if the future is regular, and that, if the future is irregular,
he conditional has the same irregularities, so that the irregular forms
f the conditional are not listed.

Of each verb, we first give the infinitive, the present participle and
he past participle, in that order, whether irregular or not, and then
he irregularities. Abbreviations:

P.I. for present indicative; **P.S.** for present subjunctive; **F.** for
uture; **I.I.** for imperfect indicative; **Imp.** for imperative.

cquérir-acquérant-acquis *(to acquire)*. P.I.: acquiers, acquiers, ac-
    quiert, acquérons, acquérez, acquièrent. P.S.: acquière, -es, -e,
    acquérions, acquériez, acquièrent. F.: acquerrai.

ller-allant-allé *(to go)*. P.I.: vais, vas, va, allons, allez, vont. P.S.:
    aille, -es, -e, allions, alliez, aillent. F.: irai. Imp.: va, allons, allez.

ppeler-appelant-appelé *(to call)*. P.I.: appelle, -es, -e, appelons,
    appelez, appellent. P.S.: appelle, appelions, appellent. F.:
    appellerai.

sseoir-asseyant (assoyant)-assis *(to sit; s'asseoir=to sit down)*. P.I.:
    assieds, assieds, assied, *or* assois, etc. P.S.: asseye *or* assoie. F.:
    asseyerai, assiérai *or* assoirai.

tteindre *(to reach, to attain)*, as **craindre.**

voir-ayant-eu *(to have)*. P.I.: ai, as, a, avons, avez, ont. P.S.: aie,
    aies, ait, ayons, ayez, aient. F.: aurai. I.I.: avais. Imp.: aie, ayons,
    ayez.

oire-buvant-bu *(to drink)*. P.I.: bois, bois, boit, buvons, buvez, boi-
    vent. P.S.: boive, -es, -e, buvions, buviez, boivent. Imp.: bois,
    buvons, buvez.

ouillir-bouillant-bouilli *(to boil)*. P.I.: bous.

omparaître *(to appear)*, as **connaître.**

omprendre *(to understand; to contain)*, as **prendre.**

onclure-concluant-conclu *(to conclude)*. P.I.: conclus.

onduire *(to guide, to conduct)*, as **cuire.**

onnaître-connaissant-connu *(to know)*. P.I.: connais, connais, con-
    naît.

onsentir *(to consent)*, as **sentir.**

onstruire *(to construct)*, as **cuire.**

ontenir *(to contain)*, as **tenir.**

onvenir *(to suit, to be convenient)*, as **venir.**

oudre-cousant-cousu *(to sew)*. P.I.: couds. Imp.: couds, cousons,
    cousez.

ourir-courant-couru *(to run)*. P.I.: cours. F.: courrai.

Couvrir-couvrant-couvert *(to cover)*. P.I.: couvre, -es, -e, couvron
couvrez, couvrent.

Craindre-craignant-craint *(to fear)*. P.I.: crains, crains, craint, crai-
gnons, craignez, craignent.

Croire-croyant-cru *(to believe)*. P.I.: crois, crois, croit, croyons, croye
croient. P.S.: croie, -es, -e, croyions, croyiez, croient. F.: croira
Imp.: crois, croyons, croyez.

Croître-croissant-crû *(to grow, to increase)*. P.I.: croîs, croîs, croî
croissons, croissez, croissent. F.: croîtrai.

Cuire-cuisant-cuit *(to cook, to bake)*. P.I.: cuis.

Découvrir *(to discover)*, as **couvrir.**

Détruire *(to destroy)*, as **cuire.**

Devoir-devant-dû, dus, due, dues *(to have to, must)*. P.I.: dois, doi
doit, devons, devez, doivent. P.S.: doive, -es, -e, devions, devie
doivent. F.: devrai.

Dire-disant-dit *(to say, to tell)*. P.I.: dis, dis, dit, disons, dites, disen
P.S.: dise, -es, -e, disions, disiez, disent.

Disparaître *(to disappear)*, as **connaître.**

Dissoudre-dissolvant-dissous, dissoute *(to dissolve)*. P.I.: dissous, di
sous, dissout, dissolvons, dissolvez, dissolvent.

Dormir-dormant-dormi *(to sleep)*. P.I.: dors, dors, dort, dormon
dormez, dorment. P.S.: dorme, -es, -e, dormions, dormiez, dormen

Ecrire-écrivant-écrit *(to write)*. P.I.: écris, écris, écrit, écrivons, écrive
écrivent. P.S.: écrive, -es, -e, écrivions, écriviez, écrivent.

Envoyer-envoyant-envoyé *(to send)*. P.I.: envoie, -es, -e, envoyon
envoyez, envoient. F.: enverrai.

Espérer-espérant-espéré *(to hope)*. P.I.: espère, -es, -e, espérons, esp
rez, espèrent.

Etre-étant-été *(to be)*. P.I.: suis, es, est, sommes, êtes, sont. P.S.: soi
sois, soit, soyons, soyez, soient. F.: serai. Imp.: sois, soyons, soye

Faire-faisant-fait *(to make, to do)*. P.I.: fais, fais, fait, faisons, faite
font. P.S.: fasse, -es, -e, fassions, fassiez, fassent. F.: ferai.

Falloir-*(lacking)***-fallu** *(to be necessary; must)*. (Used in 3rd perso
sing. only.) P.I.: faut. P.S.: faille. F.: faudra. I.I.: fallait.

Haïr-haïssant-haï *(to hate)*. P.I.: hais, hais, hait, haïssons, haïsse
haïssent.

Jeter-jetant-jeté *(to throw)*. P.I.: jette, -es, -e, jetons, jetez, jetten
P.S.: jette, -es, -e, jetions, jetiez, jettent. F.: jetterai.

Joindre-joignant-joint *(to join, to link)*. P.I.: joins, joins, joint, joi-
gnons, joignez, joignent.

Lire-lisant-lu *(to read)*. P.I.: lis, lis, lit, lisons, lisez, lisent.

Mentir-mentant-menti *(to lie)*. P.I.: mens, mens, ment, mentons, mentez, mentent.

Mettre-mettant-mis *(to put, to place)*. P.I.: mets, mets, met, mettons, mettez, mettent.

Mourir-mourant-mort *(to die)*. P.I.: meurs, meurs, meurt, mourons, mourez, meurent. P.S.: meure, -es, -e, mourions, mouriez, meurent. F.: mourrai.

Mouvoir-mouvant-mû, mus, mue, mues *(to move)*. P.I.: meus, meus, meut, mouvons, mouvez, meuvent. P.S.: meuve, -es, -e, mouvions, mouviez, meuvent.

Naître-naissant-né *(to be born)*, P.I.: as **connaître.**

Offrir-offrant-offert *(to offer)*. P.I.: offre, -es, -e, offrons, offrez, offrent.

Ouvrir *(to open)*, as **couvrir.**

Paraître *(to appear, to seem)*, as **connaître.**

Partir-partant-parti *(to leave)*. P.I.: pars, pars, part, partons, partez, partent.

Plaire-plaisant-plu *(to please)*. P.I.: plais, plais, plaît, plaisons, plaisez, plaisent.

Pleuvoir-pleuvant-plu *(to rain)*. P.I.: il pleut.

Pouvoir-pouvant-pu *(to be able to; to be allowed to)*. P.I.: peux (puis), peux, peut, pouvons, pouvez, peuvent. P.S.: puisse, -es, -e, puissions, puissiez, puissent. F.: pourrai.

    Note. Only in the first person singular of the P.I. is a distinction made between "I can" and "I may". *Je peux* is "I can" and *je puis* is "I may." The interrogative form, however, is always *puis-je.*

Prendre-prenant-pris *(to take)*. P.I.: prends, prends, prend, prenons, prenez, prennent. P.S.: prenne, -es, -e, prenions, preniez, prennent. Imp.: prends, prenons, prenez.

Produire *(to produce)*, see **cuire.**

Rire-riant-ri *(to laugh)*. P.I.: ris, ris, rit, rions, riez, rient.

Savoir-sachant-su *(to know; often: to know how to . . .)*. P.I.: sais, sais, sait, savons, savez, savent. P.S.: sache, -es, -e, sachions, sachiez, sachent. F.: saurai. I.I.: savais, savais, savait, savions, saviez, savaient. Imp.: sache, sachons, sachez.

Sentir-sentant-senti *(to feel,* in the sense of "to experience"; *to smell)*. P.I.: sens, sens, sent, sentons, sentez, sentent.

Servir-servant-servi *(to serve)*. P.I.: sers, sers, sert, servons, servez, servent.

Sortir-sortant-sorti *(to go out)*. P.I.: sors, sors, sort, sortons, sortez, sortent.

Souffrir *(to suffer)*, as **offrir.**

Suffire-suffisant-suffi *(to be sufficient)*. P.I.: suffis, suffis, suffit, suffisons, suffisez, suffisent.

Suivre-suivant-suivi *(to follow)*. P.I.: suis, suis, suit, suivons, suivez, suivent. Imp.: suis, suivons, suivez.

(Se) taire-taisant-tu *(to be silent, to keep one's mouth shut)*. P.I.: tais, tais, tait, taisons, taisez, taisent. Imp.: tais-toi, taisons-nous, taisez-vous.

Tenir-tenant-tenu *(to keep, to hold)*. P.I.: tiens, tiens, tient, tenons, tenez, tiennent. P.S.: tienne, -es, -e, tenions, teniez, tiennent. F.: tiendrai. Imp.: tiens, tenons, tenez.

Traduire *(to translate)*, as **cuire.**

Valoir-valant-valu *(to be worth)*. P.I.: vaux, vaux, vaut, valons, valez, valent. P.S.: vaille, -es, -e, valions, valiez, vaillent. F.: vaudrai.

Venir *(to come)*, as **tenir.**

Vêtir-vêtant-vêtu *(to dress, to clothe)*. P.I.: vêts, vêts, vêt, vêtons, vêtez, vêtent.

Vivre-vivant-vécu *(to live)*. P.I.: vis, vis, vit, vivons, vivez, vivent. P.S.: vive, -es, -e, vivions, viviez, vivent. Imp.: vis, vivons, vivez.

Voir-voyant-vu *(to see)*. P.I.: vois, vois, voit, voyons, voyez, voient. F.: verrai.

Vouloir-voulant-voulu *(to want, to be willing)*. P.I.: veux, veux, veut, voulons, voulez, veulent. P.S.: veuille, -es, -e, voulions, vouliez, veuillent. F.: voudrai. Imp.: veuille, veuillez (meaning "please") *and* veux, voulons, voulez (meaning "have the will to").

FRENCH-ENGLISH DICTIONARY

A

a (avoir) has
à at, to
abandonner to abandon
abeille *f.* bee
abonner, s' to subscribe
abord, d' at first
aboutir à to end in, to lead to
abréger to cut short, be brief
absent,-e absent
absenter, s' to absent oneself
abside *f.* apse
absolument absolutely
accélérateur *m.* accelerator
accent *m.* accent, stress
accepter to accept
accès interdit no trespassing
accident *m.* accident
accompagner to accompany
accord *m.* agreement
  d' . . . OK, agreed
  être d' . . . to agree
accuser to accuse
achat *m.* purchase
  faire des achats to shop
acheter to buy
acide borique *m.* boric acid
acidité *f.* acidity
acier *m.* steel
acte *m.* act
activité *f.* activity
actuel,-le present, now
actuellement at present,
  nowadays
addition *f.* bill
admiration *f.* admiration
admirer to admire
adresse *f.* address
adresser to address, to send
  s' . . . à to speak to someone

adulte grown up
aérien,-ne aerial, air
aéroport *m.* airport
affaire *f.* affair, business
  . . .s *f. pl.* business, things
affiche *f.* bill (of a theater)
affluence *f.* flow
  heure d' . . . rush hour
affranchir to free
affranchissement *m.* postage
âge *m.* age
  moyen . . . Middle Ages
âgé,-e old
agence *f.* agency
  . . .de voyages travel agency
agenda *m.* journal
agent (de police) *m.*
  policeman
agir to act
  s' . . . de to be a question of
agneau *m.* lamb
agréable agreeable, nice,
  pleasant
aider to aid, help·
aiguille *f.* needle
ail *m.* garlic
aile *f.* wing
ailleurs elsewhere
  d' . . . moreover
aimable kind, pleasant
aimer to like, to love
  . . . mieux to prefer
ainsi thus
  . . . que as well as
air *m.* air, appearance
  courant d' . . . draft
  avoir l' . . . de to look like
ajouter to add
ajusté,-e adjusted, close fitting
ajuster to adjust

alentours neighborhood
  aux . . . de in the
  neighborhood of
allemand,-e German
aller to go
  . . . bien to be well
  s'en . . . to go away
  . . . et retour round trip
  ça va that's OK
allô! hello!
allonger to lengthen
  s' . . . to lie down
allumage *m.* ignition
allumer to light, to turn the
  light on
allumette *f.* match
allure *f.* speed, clip
  à bonne . . . at a good clip
alors then, well!
altitude *f.* altitude
aluminium *m.* aluminum
amabilité *f.* kindness
âme *f.* soul
amener to bring
amer, amère bitter
américain,-e *m., f.* American
ami,-e *m., f.* friend
amidon *m.* starch
amoureux,-euse amorous
ample wide
ampoule *f.* electric light bulb
amusant,-e amusing
amuser to amuse
  s' . . . to have a good time
an *m.* year
ananas *m.* pineapple
ancêtre *m.* ancestor
ancien,-ne old, ancient, former
anglais,-e *m., f.* Englishman,
  Englishwoman, English
  (language)
Angleterre *f.* England
année *f.* year
anniversaire *m.* anniversary,
  birthday
annoncer to announce
annuaire *m.* telephone book
annuler to cancel
antiquité *f.* antiquity
août *m.* August
apercevoir to perceive

s' . . . de to realize
à peu près about
appareil *m.* device; camera
appartement *m.* apartment
appartenir to belong
appeler to call
  s' . . . to be called, named
  je m'appelle my name is
appétit *m.* appetite
apporter to bring
apprendre to learn, to teach
appris,-e learned
(s') approcher to approach, to
  come near
approfondir to go into
  deeply
appuyer to support, lean, press
après after
  . . . que after
  d' . . . according to
après-demain day after
  tomorrow
après-midi *m., f.* afternoon
arbre *m.* tree
architecte *m.* architect
argent *m.* money, silver
argenterie *f.* silverware
argot *m.* slang
aristocratique aristocratic
arme *f.* weapon
armée *f.* army
armoire *f.* wardrobe
arranger to arrange
  s' . . . to manage to
arrêt *m.* stop
(s') arrêter to stop
arrière *f.* back, rear
  à l' . . . in the rear
arrivée *f.* arrival
arriver to arrive, happen
art *m.* art
artichaut *m.* artichoke
article *m.* article
artificiel,-le artificial
artiste *m.* artist; *adj.* artistic
ascenseur *m.* elevator
asperge *f.* asparagus
aspirine *f.* aspirin
assaisonnement *m.* seasoning
assemblée *f.* assembly

asseoir, s' to sit down
assez enough, rather
assiette f. plate
assimilé assimilated
assis,-e seated
assister à to be present at, attend
assortir to sort, to match
assurance f. assurance, insurance
assurément assuredly, surely
atelier m. workshop
attacher to attach
    ... **du prix à** to set a value on something
(s') attaquer (à) to attack
attaque f. attack
attendre to wait, to wait for
    s' ... à to expect
attention! watch out!
attentivement attentively
atterrir to land (an airplane)
attirer to attract, to draw
attraper to catch
au (à+le) at the, to the
    ... **contraire** on the contrary
aube f. dawn
aucun,-e any
    ne ... not any, no, none
au-dessous under, underneath
au-dessus above, on top
augmenter to increase
aujourd'hui today
    ... **même** this very day
auparavant previously
auprès close to
    ... **de** f. near
au revoir good bye
aussi also, too
aussitôt immediately, soon
    ... **que** as soon as
autant as much, so much
auteur m. author
authentique authentic
autobus m. bus
automatique automatic
automne f. autumn
automobile f. automobile, car
autour around

autre other
autrefois formerly
autrement otherwise, differently
    ... **dit** in other words
auxquelles to which
avance f. advance
    à l' ... in advance
    en ... fast, ahead of time
avancer to advance, to be fast
avant before
avant-hier day before yesterday
avec with
aventure f. adventure
avion m. airplane
avis m. opinion, notice
aviser to warn, inform
avoir to have
    ... **l'air de** to appear
    ... **besoin** to need
    ... **faim** to be hungry
    ... **soif** to be thirsty
    ... **tort** to be wrong
    ... **chaud** to be warm
avouer to confess
avril m. April

B

bachot m. slang for baccalaureate degree bachelor's examination
bagage m. baggage
bague f. ring (on finger)
baguette f. wand
baigner, se to take a bath
baignoire f. bathtub
bail m. lease
bain m. bath
    ... **de pieds** foot bath
    ... **de soleil** sun bath
baisse f. subsidence, fall
    en ... dropping
bal m. ball (dance)
balance f. scales
ballon m. balloon
banane f. banana
bandage m. bandage
banlieue f. outskirts, suburbs
banque f. bank
bar m. bar

barbe *f.* beard
baromètre *m.* barometer
barrer to block
barrière *f.* barrier, gate
bas,-se low
bas *m.* stocking
bassin *m.* basin
bataille *f.* battle
bateau,-x *m.* ship, boat
bâtiment *m.* building
bâton *m.* stick
beau, bel, belle beautiful, fine
beaucoup much, very much
   many
   ... de much, a great deal,
   a lot of, many
beau-frère *m.* brother-in-law
beauté *f.* beauty
belge Belgian
belle-soeur *f.* sister-in-law
bénéfice *m.* profit
béret *m.* cap
besoin *m.* need
   avoir ... de to need
bête *f.* animal, stupid
beurre *m.* butter
bibliothèque *f.* library
bicyclette *f.* bicycle
bien all right, comfortable,
   very well
   ... entendu of course
   ... que although
bientôt soon
   à ... see you soon, so long
bienveillance *f.* kindness
bière *f.* beer
bijou,-x *m.* jewel
bijoutier *m.* jeweler
bijouterie *f.* jewelry
billet *m.* bill, paper money,
   ticket
   ... de passage passage, boat
   ticket
bisque *f.* shellfish soup
blague *f.* kidding (slang)
blaireau *m.* shaving brush
blanc, blanche white
blanchisserie *f.* laundry
blé *m.* wheat
bleu,-e blue
blouse *f.* blouse

bock *m.* glass of beer
boeuf *m.* beef
boire to drink
bois *m.* wood
boisson *f.* drink
boîte *f.* box
   ... de nuit *f.* night club
bon, bonne good, fine
bonhomme *m.* old fellow
bonjour good day, hello,
   good morning
bon marché cheap
bonne *f.* maid
bonsoir good evening
bonté *f.* goodness, kindness
bord *m.* edge
   ... de la mer seashore
border to border
bouche *f.* mouth
boucher *m.* butcher
boucle *f.* curl
   ... s d'oreille earrings
boue *f.* mud
bouillir to boil
boulanger *m.* baker
boulevard *m.* boulevard
bouquet *m.* bouquet
bourse *f.* stock exchange
bout *m.* end
   tout au ... at the very end
bouteille *f.* bottle
boutique *f.* shop
bouton *m.* button
   ... de manchette cuff link
boxe *f.* boxing
bracelet *m.* bracelet
bracelet-montre *m.* wrist
   watch
bras *m.* arm
brave good, brave
bredouiller to mumble
bretelles *f.* suspenders
brillant brilliant
brique *f.* brick
briquet *m.* lighter
broder to embroider
broderie *f.* embroidery
brosse *f.* brush
   ... à dents *f.* toothbrush
brouillard *m.* fog
bruit *m.* noise

brûler to burn
brumeux,-euse foggy
brun,-e brown
bulletin *m.* bulletin, report,
bureau,-x *m.* desk, office
   ... **de poste** post office
   ... **de tabac** cigar store
but *m.* goal
buvard *m.* blotter

C

ça that, this
   c'est ... that's it, O.K.
cabaret *m.* cabaret
cabine *f.* cabine
   ... **téléphonique** telephone
   booth
cabinet *m.* toilet
câble *m.* cablegram
cacahuète *f.* peanut
cadeau *m.* gift
cadre *m.* frame
café *m.* coffee, café
cahier *m.* notebook
caisse *f.* case, cash-box
caissier, caissière cashier
caleçon *m.* underdrawers,
   shorts
calendrier *m.* calendar
camion *m.* truck
campagne *f.* country,
   campaign
   à la ... in the country
   faire la ... de to go through
   the campaign of
canapé *m.* sofa
canard *m.* duck
canif *m.* penknife
canot *m.* small boat
caoutchouc *m.* rubber
   ... **s** *m.* rubbers
capitale *f.* capital (city)
capitonner to pad
capotage *m.* overturn, upset
car for
caractère *m.* character
caractéristique characteristic
carafe *f.* decanter
carapace *f.* shell
carbone *m.* carbon
carotte *f.* carrot

carré square
carreau *m.* check, square
carrément plainly
carte *f.* card
   ... **d'identité** identification
   card
   donner les ... s to deal the
   cards
   ... **des vins** wine list
carte postale illustrée *f.*
   picture postcard
cas *m.* case, circumstance
casquette *f.* cap
casser to break
cathédrale *f.* cathedral
cause *f.* cause
   a ... de because
causer to converse, to converse
   about
cave *f.* cellar, cellar club
caviar *m.* caviar
ce it, they
ce, cet, cette this, that
ceinture *f.* belt
cela that
célèbre famous
celle *f.* the one, she, it
   ... **-ci** *f.* this one
   ... **-là** that one
celui *m.* the one
   ... **-ci** *m.* this one
   ... **-là** *m.* that one
censé supposed to
cent *m.* a hundred
   pour ... per cent
centaine *f.* about a hundred
centime *m.* centime (100th
   part of a franc)
centre *m.* center
   au ... in the center
cependant however
céréale *f.* cereal
certainement certainly
cerveau *m.* brain, mind
ceux the ones, they
   ... **-ci** these
   ... **-là** those
chacun,-e each
chaise *f.* chair
chaise-longue *f.* deck-chair
chaleur *f.* heat

chambre *f.* room
   . . . à coucher bedroom
chambre meublée *f.* furnished
   room
champignon *m.* mushroom
chance *f.* luck
   bonne . . . good luck
change *m.* exchange
changer to change
chanson *f.* song
chanter to sing
chapeau,-x *m.* hat
   . . . de paille straw hat
chapelle *f.* chapel
chapitre *m.* chapter
chaque each, every
charmant,-e charming
charme *m.* charm
chasse *f.* hunt, chase
chasser to hunt, to drive away,
   to dismiss
chat *m.* cat
château *m.* castle
   . . . fort fortress
chaud,-e hot, warm
   avoir . . . to be hot, warm
   (said of a person)
   faire . . . to be hot, warm
   (said of the weather)
chauffage *m.* heating
chauffer to heat, to warm
chauffeur *m.* driver, chauffeur
chaussette *f.* sock
chaussure *f.* shoe
chef *m.* chief, chef
chemin *m.* roadway
   . . . de traverse crossroad,
   sideroad
   . . . de fer railroad
chemise *f.* shirt
   . . . de nuit *f.* nightgown
chèque *m.* check
   . . . de tourisme *m.*
   travelers check
cher, chère dear, expensive
chercher to look for
   envoyer . . . to send for
chéri,-e *m.,f.* darling
cheval *m.* horse
cheveu,-eux a hair, hair
cheville *f.* ankle

chèvre *f.* goat
chevreau *m.* kid
chez at, at the house of
   . . . Jean at John's place
   . . . lui at his place
chic fine, elegant, grand
chiffon *m.* rag
chien *m.* dog
chocolat *m.* chocolate
choisir to choose
choix *m.* choice
chose *f.* thing
chou *m.* cabbage
chou-fleur *m.* cauliflower
ciel *m.* sky
cigare *m.* cigar
cigarette *f.* cigarette
ciment *m.* cement
cinéma *m.* motion picture
   house
cinq five
cinquante fifty
cinquième fifth
circulation *f.* traffic
circuler to spread, to circulate
cirer to shine (shoes)
ciseaux *m. pl* scissors
cité *f.* city
citer to quote, to cite
citoyen,-ne citizen
citron *m.* lemon
citronnade *f.* lemonade
clair,-e clear, light
clarté *f.* clarity, light
classe *f.* class
classique classical
clavier *m.* keyboard
clef *f.* key, wrench
client *m.* customer
climat *m.* climate
clinique *f.* clinic
clou *m.* nail
coeur *m.* heart
   avoir mal au . . . to feel sick
cognac *m.* brandy
cogner to knock
coiffer to fix the hair of
   se . . . to fix one's hair
coiffeur *m.* barber,
   hairdresser
coin *m.* corner

col *m.* collar
colère *f.* anger
 en . . . angry
colis *m.* parcel
 . . . postal parcel post
collaborateur *m.* collaborator
collège *m.* college, school
colonne *f.* column
combien de how many, how much
combinaison *f.* slip
comble *m.* top, zenith
 . . . de malheur to top it all
comédie *f.* comedy
commander to order
comme as, like, since
 . . . ci, . . . ça so so
 . . . il faut proper, refined
commencement *m.* beginning
 au . . . in the beginning
commencer to begin, to start
comment how
 . . . va? how is . . . ?
commerce *m.* commerce, trade
commercial,-e business
commissariat *m.* police station
commode practical
commode *f.* dresser
communément commonly
communication *f.* communication
communiquer to communicate
compagnie *f.* company
comparaison *f.* comparison
comparer compare
compartement *m.* compartment
complet *m.* suit of clothes
complet, complète complete, full
complètement completely
complicité *f.* **agir de . . .** to act in collusion
compliment *m.* compliment
compliqué,-e complicated
composer to compose
comprendre to understand
comptabilité *f.* accounting
comptant ready, in cash
 payer au . . . to pay cash

compte *m.* account; bill
 se rendre . . . to realize
compter to expect, to count
compteur *m.* meter
concert *m.* concert
concierge *m., f.* building superintendent
conclure to conclude
conducteur *m.* driver
conduire to conduct, drive, take, lead
conduite *f.* conduct
conférence *f.* lecture
confiture *f.* jam
confort *m.* comfort
 . . . moderne modern conveniences
confortable comfortable
connaissance *f.* acquaintance, knowledge
connaissement *m.* bill of lading
connaître to be acquainted with, to know
consacrer, to devote
conscience *f.* conscience, mind
conseil *m.* advice, counsel
conservatoire *m.* conservatory
considération *f.* regard, esteem
considérer to consider
consigne *f.* checkroom (in a railroad station)
 mettre à la . . . to check (a parcel)
consister to consist
constamment constantly
constater to ascertain, observe the fact that
construire to construct, to build
construit constructed
consulat *m.* consulate
consultation *f.* consultation, visit
consulter to consult
conte *m.* story
contemporain,-e contemporary
content,-e happy

contenter to satisfy
  se ... to be satisfied
conter to relate, to tell
continental,-aux *m.*
  continental
continuer to continue
contraire contrary
  au ... on the contrary
contrarié,-e upset
contraste *m.* contrast
  faire ... to contrast
contrat *m.* contract
contre against
  par ... on the other hand
contredire to contradict
  sans contredit without
  question
contrôler to check
contrôleur *m.* ticket collector
convenable convenient
convenir to agree, to suit
convenu,-e agreed
conversation *f.* conversation
copie *f.* copy
coque *f.* shell (of egg)
coquet,-te dainty, trim
corbeille *f.* basket
cordialement cordially
cordonnier *m.* shoemaker
corps *m.* body
correspondance *f.* mail,
  correspondence
corridor *m.* corridor
corriger to correct
corsage *m.* blouse
costume *m.* suit
  ... de bain *m.* bathing
  suit
côte *f.* hill, incline, shore,
  coast
côté *m.* side
  du ... de in the direction of
  de l'autre ... on the other
  side
  à ... de beside
côtelette *f.* cutlet, chops
coton *m.* cotton
  ... hydrophile *m.*
  absorbent cotton
cou *m.* neck
coucher to lie down

se ... to go to sleep
chambre à ... *f.* bedroom
couché,-e lying down
couchette *f.* berth
coudre to sew
couleur *f.* color
coup *m.* stroke, blow
  tout à ... suddenly
  tout d'un ... suddenly
  ... de soleil *m.* sunburn
coupe *f.* haircut
couper to cut
  se ... to cut oneself
cour *f.* courtyard
couramment commonly,
  ordinarily
  parler ... to speak with
  ease, rapidly
courant current, everyday
courant *m.* current
  dans le ... de la semaine
  during the week
  être au ... de to be
  informed of
coureur *m.* runner
courir to run
couronne *f.* crown
courrier *m.* mail
cours *m.* course
course *f.* errand, race
  ... de chevaux horse race
  ... à pied foot race, track
  meet
  faire les courses to shop
court,-e short
courtisan *m.* courtier
cousin,-e *m., f.* cousin
coussin *m.* pillow
coût *m.* cost
couteau,-x *m.* knife
coûter to cost
coutume *f.* custom, habit
couture *f.* sewing, tailoring
couturier dressmaker
couvert *m.* cover, shelter
  le temps est ... the weather
  is cloudy
couverture *f.* cover, blanket
couvrir to cover
craindre to fear
cravate *f.* tie, necktie

crayon *m.* pencil
crédit *m.* credit
  à ... on credit
créer to create
crème *f.* cream, cold cream
  ... à barbe *f.* shaving
  cream
crêpe *m.* crepe
crevaison *f.* puncture
crever to blow out (said of a
  tire)
crier to shout
crise *f.* crisis
critique critical
croire to believe, to think
cru,-e believed, thought
cuillère *f.* spoon
cuir *m.* leather
cuire to cook
cuisine *f.* kitchen
cuisinière *f.* cook
cuisse *f.* leg (of meat)
cuit,-e cooked
  bien ... well cooked
culotte *f.* panties
cure dent *m.* toothpick
curieux, -euse curious, funny,
  strange
cuvette *f.* wash basin
cylindre *m.* cylinder

D

dactylographe *m. f.* typist
dame *f.* lady
damner to damn
danger *m.* danger
dangereux,-euse dangerous
dans in, into
danser dance, to
date *f.* date
davantage more
de of, from, by, with
déballage *m.* unpacking
débarquer to disembark, to
  land
de bonne heure early
debout standing, up
débrouiller,-se to manage
décembre *m.* December
déclaration *f.* statement
déclarer to declare, to bid

décoller to take off (aviation)
décolorer to bleach
décor *m.* setting
décorer to decorate
dedans inside
défaire to undo
défendre to defend, to forbid
défense d'entrer no
  admittance
défier to challenge
degré *m.* degree
déguerpir to decamp
dehors outside
déja already
déjeuner *m.* lunch
  petit ... breakfast
déjeuner to lunch, to have
  lunch
délabré,-e dilapidated
délicat,-e delicate
délicatesse *f.* delicacy
delicieux,-euse delicious
demain tomorrow
  à ... see you tomorrow
demander to ask
  se ... to wonder
déménager to move away
demeurer to live, to reside
demi,-e half
démocratie *f.* democracy
demoiselle *f.* young lady
démolir to demolish
dent *f.* tooth
dentelle *f.* lace
dentiste *m.* dentist
dépanneur *m.* service man,
  garage man
départ *m.* departure
dépasser to surpass
dépêche *f.* telegram
(se) dépêcher to hurry
dépendre to depend
dépenser to spend
déplacer to move
  se ... to move
déposer to set down,
  to deposit
depuis since, for
  ... que since
déranger to disturb, to
  inconvenience

dernier,-ère last
dérober to steal
   à la dérobée on the sly
derrière behind
des some, of the, from the
dès from
   ... que as early as, as soon as
désagréable unpleasant
descendre to go down, get off
désespéré,-e desperate
déshabiller, se to undress
désirer to desire, to wish
désolé sorry, dejected
dessert *m.* dessert
desservir to clear away the
   dishes
dessous beneath, under
dessus above, on, over
détester to dislike, to detest
destination *f.* destination
détaillé,-e detailed
détraqué,-e out of order
détromper to undeceive
dette *f.* debt
deux two
deuxième second
devant in front of, before
développer to develop
devenir to become
devoir *m.* duty, lesson
devoir to have to, to owe,
dévorer to devour
diamant *m.* diamond
différence *f.* difference
différent-e different
difficile difficult
difficulté *f.* difficulty
digestion *f.* digestion
digne worthy
dignité *m.* dignity
dimanche *m.* Sunday
dîner *m.* dinner
dîner to dine
diplôme *m.* diploma
dire to say, to tell
   à vrai ... to tell the truth
   vouloir ... to mean
direct,-e direct
directement directly
direction *f.* direction,
   management

discuter to argue, to discuss,
   to dispute
disparaître to disappear
disposer to dispose, to arrange
distance *f.* distance
distingué,-e distinguished
dit,-e said, told
divers,-e diverse, different
diviser divide
dix ten
dix-sept seventeen
docteur *m.* doctor
doigt *m.* finger
domestique *m., f.* servant
domicile *m.* home
   à ... at home
dommage *m.* damage, pity,
   c'est ... it's a pity;
   that's too bad
donc therefore
donner to give
   ... sur la rue to face the
   street
dont whose, of whom, of
   which
dormir to sleep
douane *f.* customs
   custom-house
douanier *m.* customs officer
double double
doubler to double
douche *f.* shower
douleur *f.* pain, sorrow
doute *m.* doubt
   sans ... doubtless
douter to doubt
   se ... de to suspect
doux, douce sweet
douzaine *f.* dozen
douze twelve
dramaturge *m.* dramatist
drap *m.* sheet
(se) dresser to rise up
droit,-e right
   à ... on the right
drôle funny
du (de+le) some
duc *m.* duke
dur,-e tough, hard
durer to last

E

eau *f.* water
  ... **courante** running water
  ... **gazeuse** *f.* soda water
  ... **minérale** *f.* mineral
    water
éblouir to dazzle
échange *m.* exchange
échelle *f.* ladder
éclair *m.* lightning
éclairer to light up
éclatant,-e brilliant
école *f.* school
écouter to listen (to)
écrevisse *f.* crayfish
écrire to write
écrit,-e written
écriteau *m.* sign
écrivain *m.* writer
édifice *m.* building
édition *f.* edition, publication
effet *m.* effect
  en ... that's true
effets *m.* clothes, personal
  effects
égal,-e equal
  être ... to make no difference
égarer to mislay
  s' ... to lose one's way
église *f.* church
égratignure *f.* scratch
eh bien! well!
électricité *f.* electricity
électrique electric
élégant,-e elegant
élève *m., f.* student, pupil
élevé,-e high
élever to lift, to raise
élire to elect
elle she, it, her
elles *f.* they, them
emballer to pack
embêtant,-e annoying
embarquer to embark, to sail
embouteillage *m.* traffic jam
embrasser to kiss
embrouiller to mix up
  s' ... to get mixed up
emmener to take along

empaqueter to pack up
empêcher to prevent
empeser to starch
emplacement *m.* site
employé,-e *m., f.* employee
emporter to carry off
empresser, s' to hurry
en in, into, of it, of them,
  some, by, on, upon, while
enchanté,-e charmed, delighted
encore yet, still
  pas ... not yet
encre *f.* ink
encrier *m.* inkstand
endormir, s' go to sleep
endroit *m.* place, spot
enfance *f.* childhood
enfant *m., f.* child
enfer *m.* hell
enfermer to shut up
enfin finally
engrais *m.* fertilizer
ennuyer to annoy, to bother
  s' ... to be bored
énorme enormous
énormément enormously
enraciné deeply rooted
enregistrer to check (baggage);
  to register (a letter)
en retard late
ensemble together
enseigner to teach
ensuite then, afterwards
entendre to hear
  ... **dire** to hear (say)
entendu,-e heard, agreed
  bien ... of course
enthousiasme *m.* enthusiasm
entier,-ère entire
entourer to surround
entre among, between
entr'acte *m.* intermission
entrée *f.* entrance
entrer to enter
  ... **dans** to enter
  ... **en relation** to get in
  touch
enveloppe *f.* envelope
envelopper to wrap up
envers towards
envie *f.* fancy, desire

environs *m.pl.* surroundings, vicinity
en voiture! all aboard!
envoyer to send
  . . . **chercher** to send for
épatant,-e swell, fine
épaule *f.* shoulder
épicerie *f.* grocery store
épicier, épicière *m., f.* grocer
épingle *f.* pin
épique *adj.* epic
éponge *f.* sponge
époque *f.* epoch
épreuve *f.* print
éprouver to experience, to feel, to test
erreur *f.* error, mistake
escalier *m.* stairway
(s') esclaffer to burst out laughing
espagnol,-e Spanish
espèce *f.* kind
espérer to hope
essayer to try, try on
essence *f.* gasoline
est *m.* east
estimer to value
estomac *m.* stomach
estropier to cripple
et and
établir to establish
étage *m.* floor, story
étain *m.* tin
état *m.* state, condition
Etats-Unis *m.pl.* United States
été *m.* summer
éteindre to extinguish, turn light off
éternité *f.* eternity
étoffe *f.* cloth
étoile *f.* star
étouffer to suffocate
étrange strange
étranger, étrangère foreign
etranger,-ère foreigner
être to be
  . . . **à la page** to be up to date
  . . . **au courant de** to be informed, to be aware of

  . . . **en train de** to be in the act of, to be engaged in
étroit,-e narrow, tight
étude *f.* study
étudiant,-e student
étudier to study
européen,-ne European
eux they, them
évanouir, s' to faint
évènement *m.* event
evidemment obviously
évier *m.* sink
éviter to avoid
exact,-e exact
examen *m.* examination
examiner to examine
excepté except
exception *f.* exception
  à l'. . . de with the exception of
exercer to exercise, train
excercice *m.* exercise, drill
excursion *f.* excursion
excuser to excuse
exemplaire *m.* duplicate, copy
exemplaire *adj.* exemplary
exemple *m.* example
  par . . . for example
exercer, s' to practice
expérience *f.* experience
experimenté,-e experienced
explication *f.* explanation
expliquer to explain
exportation *f.* export
exporter to export
exprès on purpose
express *m.* express train
exprimer to express
extraordinaire extraordinary
extrême extreme

F

fabrication *f.* manufacturing
fabriquer to manufacture
face *f.* face
  en . . . across the street
fâché,-e angry
fâcher to make angry
  se . . . to become angry
facile easy

façon *f.* manner, way
  de cette ... in this way
  de ... que so that
  d'une ... générale in a general way
facteur *m.* postman
factice artificial
facture *f.* bill (to be paid)
faible weak
faim *f.* hunger
  avoir ... to be hungry
faire to do, to make
  ... attention to pay attention, to be careful
  ... beau to be fine weather
  ... chaud to be hot, warm
  ... froid to be cold
  ... mal à to hurt
  ... peur à to frighten
  ... plaisir to please
  ... du soleil to be sunny
  ... du vent to be windy
  ... la toilette to get ready (dressed)
  ... le compte to draw up a bill
  ... les bagages to pack for a trip
  ... une promenade to take a walk
  ... un tour to take a walk
  se ... to become
  s'en ... to worry
  s'y ... to become used to
fait *m.* deed, fact
  au ... to the point
  en ... de as regards
falloir to be necessary, to have to, must
fameux,-euse famous
famille *f.* family
fatigué,-e tired
fatiguer to tire
  se ... to get tired
faute *f.* fault, mistake
fauteuil *m.* armchair
faux, fausse false, wrong
favori, favorite favorite
fée *f.* fairy
félicitation *f.* congratulation
femme *f.* wife, woman

... de chambre *f.* chambermaid
... de journée charwoman
fenêtre *f.* window
fer *m.* iron
  chemin de ... railroad
  ... à cheval horseshoe
fermer to close, to shut
fermeture *f.* closing, closing time, fastening
  ... éclair *f.* zipper
fête *f.* festival
feu *m.* fire
feuille *f.* leaf
  ... de papier sheet of paper
feutre *m.* felt, felt hat
février *m.* February
fiancé,-e betrothed
fièvre *f.* fever, temperature
figurer, se to imagine
fil *m.* thread
filer to ride (fast)
filet *m.* fillet
fille *f.* daughter
  petite ... little girl
film *m.* film, moving picture
fils *m.* son
filtre *m.* filter
fin *f.* end
finir to finish
flanelle *f.* flannel
flatter to flatter
flèche *f.* arrow, spire
fleur *f.* flower
fleuriste *m.,f.* florist
flottant,-e floating
flotter to float
foie *m.* liver
foire *f.* fair, market
fois *f.* time (in the sense of occurrence)
  à la ... at once, at the same time
  une ... once
  deux ... twice
foncé,-e dark
fonctionner to function, to work
fond *m.* bottom
fonds *m.pl.* funds
fontaine *f.* fountain

football *m.* football
forcer to force
formalité *f.* formality
forme *f.* form
   en . . de in the form of
former to form
   se . . . to be made up
   (said of a train)
formule *f.* formula
fort,-e strong, much, very
   much, hard
fou, fol, folle crazy
foule *f.* crowd
fourchette *f.* fork
fourneau *m.* stove
   . . . à gaz gas stove
fourrure *f.* fur
foyer *m.* lounge, lobby,
   hearth
frais, fraîche fresh, cool
fraise *f.* strawberry
franc, franche frank, sincere
franc *m.* franc (French
   monetary unit)
France *f.* France
français,-e *m.,f.* Frenchman,
   Frenchwoman, French
frapper to hit, strike, knock
frein *m.* brake
fréquenter to frequent
frère *m.* brother
frire to fry
froid,-e cold
froisser to wrinkle, to
   crumple, to offend
fromage *m.* cheese
frontière *f.* border
fruit *m.* fruit
fumée *f.* smoke
fumer to smoke
fumeur *m.* smoking
   compartment
fuselage *m.* fuselage
fur *m.* rate
   au . . . et à mesure
   progressively
future *m.* future

G

gaffe *f.* social, error, blunder
gagner to earn, to win

gai,-e gay
gaine *f.* girdle
galerie *f.* gallery, department
   store
gallo-romain Gallo-Roman
gant *m.* glove
garage *m.* garage
garantir to guarantee
garçon *m.* boy, waiter
garder to keep
gardien *m.* guardian
gare *f.* railroad station
gare *interj.* beware!
   . . . à vous watch out
garniture *f.* trimming
gastronomie *f.* gastronomy
gâteau,-x *m.* cake
gâter to spoil
gauche *f.* left
   à . . . to the left
gaufre *f.* waffle
gaz *m.* gas
gelée *f.* frost
geler to freeze
gendarme *m.* policeman
général general
genou *m.* knee
gens *m.* people
gentil,-le nice, kind
géométrique geometric
gérant *m.* manager
gilet *m.* vest
glace *f.* mirror, ice cream,
   ice, pane
glacé,-e iced
glacer to ice, freeze
glacière *f.* ice-box
gloire *f.* glory
golf *m.* golf
gomme *f.* eraser
gorge *f.* throat
   avoir mal à la . . . to have a
   sore throat
gothique Gothic
goût *m.* taste
goûter to taste, enjoy
gouvernement *m.* government
gracieux,-euse graceful
grade *m.* degree
grand,-e big, great, large
grandement greatly

grandeur *f.* size, bigness
gras,-se fat
gratte-ciel *m.* skyscraper
gratter to scratch, scrape
grec,-que Greek
grève *f.* strike (of labor)
groom *m.* bell-boy
gros, grosse big, fat
grotte *f.* cave
guère not much
  ne . . . hardly, scarcely
guérir to cure
guerre *f.* war
guichet *m.* box office
guide *m.* guide
guider to guide

H

habillement *m.* clothing
habiller, s' to dress (oneself)
habit *m.* clothes, garb
habitant *m.* inhabitant
habiter to live, dwell
habitude *f.* custom, habit
  d' . . . usually
habituer, s' to get
  accustomed to
halte *f.* halt
hameau *m.* hamlet
haricot *m.* bean
harmonieux,-euse harmonious
hausse *f.* rise (in prices)
haut,-e high
  en . . . upstairs, above
haut *m.* top
hauteur *f.* height
hélas! alas!
héler to hail
hélices *f. pl.* propellers
herbe *f.* grass
hésiter to hestitate
heure *f.* hour, o'clock
  à l' . . . on time
  c'est l' . . . it's time
  de bonne . . . early
  tout à l' . . . shortly
heureusement fortunately
heureux, heureuse happy,
  fortunate

hier yesterday
histoire *f.* history
historiographe *m.*
  historiographer
historique historical
hiver *m.* winter
homard *m.* lobster
homme *m.* man
honneur *m.* honor
honoraires *m.* fee
honorer to honor
hôpital *m.* hospital
horaire *m.* timetable
horloge *f.* public clock
horloger *m.* watchmaker
horlogerie *f.* watchmaker's
  shop
hors d'oeuvre *m.* relish
hôtel *m.* hotel
  . . . de ville city hall
huile *f.* oil
humain,-e human
humidité *f.* humidity

I

ici here
  par . . . this way
idée *f.* idea
ignorer to be unaware of
il he, it
  . . . y a there is, there are
île *f.* island
illustre illustrious
ils they
image *f.* picture
imaginer to imagine
imberbe beardless
immédiat,-e immediate
immédiatement immediately
immeuble *m.*
  apartment building
immobile still, quiet
impasse *f.* dead end
impatient-e impatient
imperméable *m.* raincoat
importance *f.* importance
importe, n' anything; it
  does not matter; I don't care
importer import, to
impossible impossible

  * An asterisk before the following words indicates that the *h* is
aspirate, allowing no elision or liaison.

impôt *m.* tax
    ... sur le revenu income tax
imprégner to impregnate
impressionant,-e impression
impressioner to impress
imprévu,-e unforeseen
inconnu,-e unknown
indicateur *m.* timetable
indiquer to indicate, to tell
indirect,-e indirect
individuel,-le individual
inférieur,-e inferior, lower
infini infinite
infiniment infinitely
infirmière *f.* nurse
information *f.* information
informer to inform
ingénieur *m.* engineer
injure *f.* insult
innombrable countless,
    innumerable
inonder to inundate
inquiéter, s' to become
    worried
inscrire to inscribe, write
    down
    se faire ... to register
    s' ... à to enroll in
insecticide *m.* insect repellent
insister to insist
installer to install, to settle
    s' ... to move in
instant *m.* instant, moment
    à l'... just now
instantané *m.* snapshot
institut *m.* institute
intellectuel,-le intellectual
intelligence *f.* intelligence
intention *f.* intention,
    purpose
interdit forbidden
intéressant,-e interesting
intérêt *m.* interest
intérieur,-e interior
interprète *m.* interpreter
intersection *f.* crossing
interurbain,-e long distance
intrépide intrepid
introduction *f.* introduction
intrus *m.* intruder
inutile useless

invitation *f.* invitation
invité *m.* guest
invité invited
inviter to invite
ironique ironical
irréel,-le unreal
italien Italian
itinéraire *m.* itinerary

J

jamais never
jambe *f.* leg
jambon *m.* ham
janvier *m.* January
jaquette *f.* jacket
jardin *m.* garden
jaune yellow
je I
jeu *m.* game
    vieux ... old fashioned
jeudi *m.* Thursday
jeune young
jeunesse *f.* youth, young
    people
joie *f.* joy
joli,-e pretty
jouer to play
    ... de to play (an
    instrument)
    ... à to play (a game)
joueur *m.* player
jouir de to enjoy
jouet *m.* toy
joujou,-x *m.* toy
jour *m.* day
    ... de congé holiday
journal,-aux *m.* newspaper
journalisme *m.* journalism
journée *f.* day
juillet *m.* July
juin *m.* June
jupe *f.* skirt
jupon *m.* petticoat
jusque until
jusqu'à till, until
jusqu'à ce que until
jusque-là up to then
juste just, exactly
    au ... exactly
justement just, precisely
justice *f.* justice

K

kilo *m.* kilogram
kilogramme *m.* kilogram
kilomètre *m.* kilometer
kiosque *m.* newsstand,
  pavillion

L

la *f.* the, her, it
là there
  ... bas over there
  ... haut up there
lac *m.* lake
lacet *m.* lace
laid,-e ugly
laideur *f.* ugliness
laine *f.* wool
laisser to leave, to let
lait *m.* milk
laitue *f.* lettuce
lame *f.* blade
  ... à rasoir *f.* razor blade
lampe *f.* lamp
lancer to throw, to hurl
langouste *f.* crayfish
langue *f.* language, tongue
lapin *m.* rabbit
lard *m.* fat
  le petit ... bacon
large broad, wide
lavabo *m.* wash basin
laver to wash
  se ... to wash oneself
le *m.* the, him, it
leçon *f.* lesson
lecture *f.* reading
léger, légère *adj.* light
légume *m.* vegetable
lendemain *m.* next day
lentement slowly
**lequel, laquelle, lesquels,
  lesquelles** who, which one
les *pl.* the, them
lettre *f.* letter
  ... recommandée registered
  letter
  ... de crédit *f.* letter of
  credit
leur their, them
  le ... theirs

lever to raise
  se ... to get up
lèvre *f.* lip
liaison liaison, connection
liberté *f.* freedom, liberty
librairie *f.* bookstore
libre free, vacancy
licence *f.* master's degree
liège *m.* cork
lieu *m.* place
  au ... de in place of
ligne *f.* line
limonade *f.* lemonade
linge dè corps *m.* underwear
lire to read
lit *m.* bed
  ... à deux places *m.* double
  bed
  ... jumeaux *m.* twin beds
litière *f.* litter
littéraire *f.* literary
littérature *f.* literature
livraison *f.* delivery, shipment
livre *m.* book
  ... des recettes cash book
livre *f.* pound
livrer to deliver
loger to lodge
loi *f.* law
loin far
lointain,-e distant
long,-ue long
longtemps longtime
lorsque when
louer to rent, to praise
loup *m.* wolf
  avoir une faim de ... to be
  dying of hunger
lourd heavy
loyer *m.* rent
lui he, her, him, to her, **to**
  him, to it
lumière *f.* light
lundi *m.* Monday
lune *f.* moon
  ... de miel honeymoon
lunettes *f.* eye glasses

M

M. Mr.
ma my

machine *f.* machine
  ...à coudre sewing machine
  ...à écrire typewriter
Madame, Mme Madam, Mrs.
mademoiselle Miss
magasin *m.* store
magique *adj.* magic
magnifique magnificent
mai *m.* May
main *f.* hand
maintenant now
  dès ... beginning now
mairie *f.* town hall
mais but
maison *f.* house
  ...de commerce business
  firm
majesté *f.* majesty
majestueusement majestically
mal badly
  pas ... enough, rather well
mal *m.* harm, evil
  ...à la gorge *m.* sore throat
  ...à la tête *m.* headache
  ...aux dents *m.* toothache
  ...au ventre *m.* stomach-
  ache
malade *m.,f.* sick person, sick
  ...imaginaire
  hypochondriac
maladie *f.* sickness
malentendu *m.*
  misunderstanding
malgré in spite of
malheur *m.* unhappiness
malheureusement
  unfortunately
malheureux, malheureuse
  m., f. unfortunate
malle *f.* trunk
malsain,-e unhealthy
maman *f.* mother
manche *f.* sleeve
manchette *f.* cuff
mandat-poste *m.* money order
manger to eat
manicure *m.* manicurist
manque *m.* lack
manquer to miss
  ...de to lack, to be out of
manteau *m.* coat

marchand *m.* merchant
marchander bargain, to
marchandise *f.* merchandise
marche *f.* walking
marché *m.* market
  bon ... cheap
marcher to go, to walk
  le faire ... make it work
mardi *m.* Tuesday
mari *m.* husband
mariage *m.* marriage,
marque *f.* mark, brand
mars *m.* March
massage facial face massage
matelas *m.* mattress
matériel *m.* equipment
matin *m.* morning
matinée *f.* morning,
mauvais,-e bad
me me, to me, myself
méchant,-e bad, unimportant
médecin *m.* physician
médecine *f.* medicine
  (profession)
médicament *m.* medicine (as
  prescribed by a physician)
médisance *f.* slander
mélange *m.* mixture
mélanger to mix
melon *m.* melon
membre *m.* member
même same, even, self
  de ... likewise
  de ... que just as
mémoire *f.* memory
  avoir bonne ... to have a
  good memory
mener to lead
mensonge *m.* lie
menton *m.* chin
menu *m.* menu
mer *m.* sea
merci thanks
mercredi *m.* Wednesday
mère *f.* mother
merveilleux, merveilleuse
  marvellous, wonderful
mes my
mesdames *f.* ladies
message *m.* message
messieurs gentlemen

mesure f. measure
metal m. metal
métro subway
mettre to place, to put, to put on
  se ... à to start
  se ... au courant de to become familiar with
  se ... en to dress in
meuble m. piece of furniture
meubler to furnish
miche f. loaf
midi m. noon
miel m. honey
mien, mienne mine
mieux better
  le ... the best
milieu m. middle
  au beau ... in the very middle
mille a thousand
mine f. appearance
  avoir mauvaise ... to look bad
minuit m. midnight
minute f. minute
miroir m. mirror
misère f. misery, poverty
mode f. fashion, style
moderne modern
modiste f. milliner
moi I, me, to me
moindre least
moins less
  à ... que unless
  au ... at least
  du ... at least
  ... cher cheaper
mois m. month
moiteur f. moistness
moitié f. half
molle soft
moment m. moment
  en ce ... now
mon, ma, mes my
mondain wordly
monde m. people, world
  tout le ... everybody
monnaie f. currency, small change
monsieur mister, sir

monter to go up, climb
montre f. watch
  ... en or goldwatch
montrer to show
monument m. public or historic building
moquer to mock
  se ... de to make fun of
morceau m. bit, piece
mordre to bite
mort f. death
mort,-e dead
mot m. word
moteur m. engine
mouche f. fly
mouchoir m. handkerchief
mouillé,-e wet
mourir to die
moustache f. moustache
moustique m. mosquito
moutarde f. mustard
mouvement m. movement
mouton m. sheep
moyen average
munir to furnish, supply
mur m. wall
musée m. museum
musicien, musicienne m., f. musician
musique f. music
mystérieux, mystérieuse mysterious

N

nage f. swimming
nager to swim
naissance f. birth
nappe f. tablecloth
nature f. nature
nature adj. plain
naturel,-le natural
naturellement naturally
néanmoins nevertheless
néccessaire necessary
ne ... pas not
ne ... que only
ne ... rien not anything, nothing
nef f. nave
neige f. snow
neiger to snow

n'est-ce pas? isn't it so?
net,-te clear, net
nettoyer to clean
    ... à sec to dry clean
neuf,-ve new
neuf nine
neveu m. nephew
ni neither
noblesse f. nobility
noir,-e black
noix f. nut
    ... de coco cocoanut
nom m. name
nombre m. number
non no, not
non plus neither
nord m. north
nos our
notaire m. notary
notamment notably
notre our
nous we, us, to us, ourselves
nous-mêmes ourselves
nouveau, nouvel, nouvelle
    new (different)
    de nouveau again, anew
nouvelle f. news, short story
novembre m. November
nuance f. shade of meaning,
    subtle difference
nuire to be hurtful, injurious
nuit f. night
numéro m. number
    ... d'appel phone number

O

obélisque m. obelisk
objectif,-ive objective
objet m. object, thing
obliger to oblige
obscurité f. obscurity,
    darkness
observation f. observation
obtenir to obtain, to get
occupant m. occupant
occupation f. business,
    occupation
occupé,-e busy
occuper to occupy
    s' ... de to take care of,

to be busy with
octobre m. October
octogonal octagonal
oeil m. eye
odeur f. odor, smell
oeuf m. egg
    ... à la coque soft-boiled
    egg
    ... sur le plat fried egg
oeuvre f. work
offenser to offend
officiel,-le official
offre f. offer
offrir to offer
oignon m. onion
oiseau m. bird
ombre f. shadow
ombrelle f. parasol
omelette f. omelet
omettre to omit
on one, they, we, you
oncle m. uncle
onde f. wave
onduler (les cheveux) wave
    (the hair)
ongle m. fingernail
    faire les ... s manicure the
    nails
onze eleven
opéra m. opera
opinion f. opinion
opposer to oppose
or m. gold
orage m. storm
orange f. orange
ordonnance f. prescription
    (of a doctor)
ordre m. order
oreille f. ear
    boucle d' ... s earrings
oreiller m. pillow
organiser to organize
orienter to incline; to tend
    s' ... to move towards,
    to direct oneself
originalité f. originality
os m. bone
oser to dare
ou or
où where

oublier to forget
ouest *m.* west
oui yes
outre-mer beyond the sea
ouvert,-e open
ouvrage *m.* work
ouvrir to open

P

paiement *m.* payment
pain *m.* bread
  petit ... roll
pair *m.* peer
paire *f.* pair
paix *f.* peace
palais *m.* palace, palate
  ... de justice court house
pâle pale
pamplemousse *m.* grapefruit
panne *f.* breakdown (of an
  automobile)
pansement *m.* dressing (*med.*)
pantalon *m.* trousers
pantoufles *f.* bedroom
  slippers
papeterie *f.* stationery store
papier *m.* paper
  ... à lettres writing paper
  ... carbone *m.*
  carbon paper
paquet *m.* package
par by, per
  ... an a year, per year
  ... jour a day, per day
  ... semaine a week, per
  week
  ... avion by air mail
paraître to appear
parapluie *m.* umbrella
parc *m.* park
parce que because
pardessus *m.* overcoat
pardon *m.* pardon
pardonner to pardon
pareil,-le same, similar, such a
parent *m.* parent
parent,-e relative
paresse *f.* laziness
paresseux,-euse lazy
parfait,-e perfect
parfaitement perfectly

parfois sometimes
parfum *m.* perfume
parisien,-ne Parisian
parler to speak
parmi among, between
parole *f.* word
part *f.* part, share
  à ... except for
  d'autre ... on the other
  hand
  quelque ... somewhere
participer to participate
particulier,-ère private
partie *f.* part
  faire ... de to be part of
partir to depart, to go away,
  to leave
  à ... de beginning with
partout everywhere
parvenir to reach
pas *m.* step, pace
  au ... de course at a run
pas not
  ... du tout not at all
passeport *m.* passport
passer to pass, to spend (time)
  se ... to take place
  se ... de to do without
passerelle *f.* gangplank
passionant,-e exciting
pâte *f.* paste
  ... dentifrice tooth paste
pâté meat paste
  ... de foie gras goose-liver
  paste
patiner to skate
pâtisserie *f.* pastry
pâtissier,-ère *m., f.* pastrymaker
patriote *m.* patriot
patron *m.* pattern, boss
paume *f.* palm (of the hand)
pauvre poor
pavillon *m.* pavilion
payer to pay
pays *m.* country
paysage *m.* scenery (in the
  countryside)
peau *f.* skin
  y laisser sa ... not to come
  out alive

pêche f. peach
peigne m. comb
peindre to paint
peine f. pain, trouble
  à ... hardly, scarcely
  avoir de la ... to have
  trouble, difficulty
peinture f. painting
pellicule f. film negative
pendant during
pendule f. wall clock
pénétrer to penetrate
pensée f. thought
penser to think
  ... à to think of (about)
  ... de to think of (have an
  opinion of)
pension f. boarding-house
  ... complète board and
  room
pente f. slope
percevoir to perceive
perdre to lose
père m. father
perfectionner, se to improve
périr to perish
permanente f. permanent
  wave
permettre to permit
perruque f. wig
personnage m. character
personne f. person
personnel,-e personal
perspective f. vista
persuader to persuade
peser to weigh
petit,-e little, small
pétrole m. petroleum
  roi du ... oil baron
peu little
  à ... près about, almost
  un tout petit ... very little
peur f. fear
  avoir ... to be afraid
peut-être perhaps
pharmacie f. pharmacy,
  drugstore
pharmacien m. pharmacist,
  druggist
photo f. photograph
phrase f. sentence

piano m. piano
pièce f. play, room
  ... d'identité identification
  paper
pied m. foot
piéton m. pedestrian
pilote m. pilot
pilule f. pill
pipe f. pipe
pire worse
  le ... the worst
pis worse
  le ... the worst
pittoresque picturesque
placard m. poster
place f. seat, square
placer to place, to put, to
  invest
plafond m. ceiling
plage f. beach
plaindre to pity
plaire to please
plaisanter to joke
plaisanterie f. joke
plaisir m. pleasure
plan m. map (of a city)
planche f. board
plancher m. floor
plante f. plant
plat m. dish, course
plat,-e flat
plateau m. tray
plate-forme f. platform
plein,-e full
pleuvoir to rain
pli m. fold
plonger to dive
pluie f. rain
plume f. pen
plupart f. majority, most
plus more, most
  au ... at most
plusieurs several
plutôt rather
pneu m. tire
pneumatique m. special
  delivery letter (delivered by
  underground pneumatic
  tube in Paris)
poche f. pocket
poème m. poem

SPECIAL OFFER

to buyers of this book:

FREE RECORD

Starts You Speaking

SPANISH OR FRENCH.....

Also GERMAN, ITALIAN, JAPANESE BRAZILIAN, Modern GREEK ARABIC, RUSSIAN and ENGLISH

VEST POCKET SPANISH—or French, German, Italian— brings you as basic an understanding of the language as is possible in book form. However, you may want to go beyond the scope of this book. You may wish to CONTINUE until you can speak and understand the language "LIKE A NATIVE." To really master a language you must HEAR it spoken, "pick up" the correct accent and rhythm of the language BY EAR! To show you how you can now learn to speak perfect Spanish (or French, German, Italian), the Institute will arrange a FREE DEMONSTRATION, right in your own home via this interesting record, of a remarkable "Learn-by-Listening" Record Course.

(Please turn over)

Why We Make This Generous Offer

There are three important reasons why the Institute for Language Study is pleased to make this special Free Record and Sample Lesson offer:

First, never before have there been so many fascinating opportunities open to those who speak foreign languages fluently. Besides the cultural and travel benefits, there are many practical dollars-and-cents advantages—and an ever-increasing number of interesting, well-paying jobs.

The Natural Method

Second, our long experience in the language field has convinced us that the "learn-by-listening" method is the fastest, most convenient and most effective method. It enables you to learn *naturally*—the way you learned English as a child. You acquire a perfect accent and perfect grammar—because that's all you hear.

Just Listen—and Learn

Finally, our professional standing in the field of languages has enabled us to make these generous arrangements with one of the foremost language schools—the inventors of the "learn-by-listening" method. And we are pleased to provide this service for those of our students who want to speak and understand a foreign language "like a native."

There is no obligation and *no salesman will call.* Just mail the card TODAY for your FREE Record.

What Others Say:

Bob Hope says... "I am studying the course in French ... I think it's a great way to study a language."

Enjoyed by Children "It is surprising how much our two children have absorbed by listening."
—Mrs. C.M.J.

"A Good Investment" "Just returned from Mexico ... Course good investment!"
—Phillips B. Iden

Institute for Language Study
71 Plymouth Street, Montclair, N.J. 07042

⬇ CLIP AND MAIL THIS COUPON TO: ⬇

INSTITUTE FOR LANGUAGE STUDY Dept. HVP #9876
71 Plymouth Street, Montclair, N. J. 07042

Gentlemen:
Please have the originators of the famous "learn-by-listening" method send me, FREE, the Sample Record and Lesson in the one language checked below—also information which describes fully the complete course and method.

(Please check FREE Language Record and Lesson you wish)

☐ Spanish ☐ French ☐ German ☐ Italian ☐ Brazilian-Portuguese
☐ Russian ☐ Japanese ☐ Modern Greek ☐ English (for Spanish-or
☐ Arabic   Portuguese-speaking people)

Name _____

Address _____

City _____ State _____

Zip Code _____ Phone _____

BK HVP/54321

BUSINESS REPLY CARD

FIRST CLASS   PERMIT NO. 1103   Montclair, N.J.

POSTAGE WILL BE PAID BY ADDRESSEE

Institute for Language Study
71 Plymouth Street
Montclair, NJ 07042

NO POSTAGE
NECESSARY
IF MAILED
IN THE
UNITED STATES

poésie *f.* poetry
poète *m.* poet
poétique poetic
poids *m.* weight
point *m.* point
   ... de vue point of view
pointure *f.* size
poire *f.* pear
poireaux *m. pl.* leeks
poisson *m.* fish
poivre *m.* pepper
poli,-e polite
police *f.* police
politique political
pomme *f.* apple
pomme de terre *f.* potato
   ... en purée mashed potato
pompe *f.* pump
pont *m.* bridge
porc *m.* pork
porche *f.* porch (church
   architecture)
port *m.* harbor, port
porte *f.* door
   ... cochère carriage gateway
porte-couteau *m.* knife rest
portefeuille *m.* bill-fold
porte-monnaie *m.* change
   purse
porte-plume *m.* fountain pen
porter to carry, to wear
   se ... bien to be well
porteur *m.* porter
portière *f.* car door
portillon *m.* wicket (gate)
portion *f.* share, helping
poser to place, to put,
   ... une question to ask a
   question
position *f.* position
posséder to possess
possible possible
poste *m.* position
poste *f.* post office
poste aérienne *f.* airmail
poste restante *f.* general
   delivery
postérité *f.* posterity
potage *m.* soup
poudre *f.* powder

poudrer to powder
   se ... to powder one's face
poule au riz *f.*
   chicken fricassee
poulet *m.* chicken
pouls *m.* pulse
poumon *m.* lung
pour for, in order to
pourboire *m.* tip
pourquoi why
poursuivre to pursue,
   to continue
pourtant however,
   nevertheless
pousser to push, to grow
pouvoir to be able
pratique practical
préalablement previously
préciser to specify
préfecture *f.* departmental
   capital
préfecture de police police
   headquarters
préférer to prefer
préjugé prejudice
premier,-ère first
prendre to take
   ... par to follow
   se ... à to go about (doing
   something)
préparer to prepare
près near
   ... de near
   de ... close up
présent *m.* present
   à ... now
présenter to present
présomptueux, -euse
   presumptuous
presque almost, nearly
presser to hurry
prêt,-e ready
prétendre to pretend, to claim
prêter to lend
prévenir to give notice,
   to warn
prier to beg, pray
primer to take precedence
principal,-e principal, main
printemps *m.* spring

privé,-e private
prix *m.* price, prize
  à des . . . raisonnables
  reasonably priced
problème *m.* problem
prochain,-e next
procuration *f.* power of
  attorney
procurer to procure
  se . . . to obtain
produire to produce
  . . . se to come forward
produit *m.* product
professeur *m.* professor,
  teacher
professionel,-le professional
profiter to take advantage of
profond,-e profound
programme *m.* program
projet *m.* plan
promenade *f.* promenade
  . . . en voiture ride
  faire une . . . to take a walk
promener to promenade,
  to take for a walk
  se . . . à cheval to go horse-
  back riding
  se . . . à pied to walk
  se . . . en auto to take a ride
promettre to promise
propos *m.* subject;
  à . . . by the way
propre clean, own
proprement properly
  . . . dit properly so-called
propriété *f.* property
proscrire to proscribe
protestation *f.* protest
prouver to prove
prune *f.* plum
puis then, moreover
puisque since
pyjamas *m.* pyjamas

Q

quai *m.* pier, dock, platform
  (of a station)
qualité *f.* quality
quand when
  . . . même just the same
quant à as to, as for

quart *m.* quarter
  . . . d'heure quarter-hour
quartier *m.* section (of a city)
quatorze fourteen
quatre four
quatrième fourth
que that, what, which, whom
  ce . . . that, which what, than
  ne . . . only
quel, quelle, quels, quelles
  what, which
quelque any, some
quelquefois sometimes
quelques-uns,-unes a few,
  some
qu'est-ce que? what
  . . . 'il y a? what is it?
  what's the matter?
question *f.* question
qui who? whom? that, which
  ce . . . that, which, what
quinzaine *f.* fortnight
quinze fifteen
quitter to leave, to quit
quoi? what?
  il n'y a pas de . . . don't
  mention it

R

raccommoder to mend
raccrocher to hang up
raconter to tell (about),
  relate
radiateur *m.* radiator
radio *f.* radio
rafraîchir to refresh, to cool
rafraîchissement refreshment
raisin *m.* grapes
raison *f.* reason, right
  avoir . . . to be right
raisonnable reasonable
raisonner to reason
ralentir to slow down
ramener to bring back
rang *m.* row; rank
rapide fast
rappeler to recall
  se . . . to remember
rapporter to bring back
rapprocher, se to draw
  closer to

raser to shave
rasoir *m.* razor
rassurer to reassure
rayonne *f.* rayon
réagir to react
réaliste realistic
recaler to flunk (reject in an examination)
récemment recently
recevoir to receive
réciter to tell, recite
recommander to recommend
   ... **une lettre** register a letter
reconnaissant grateful
reconnaître to recognize
reçu receipt
récupérer to recover
réduire to reduce
réel,-le real
réellement really
refaire to remake
refuser to refuse
regarder to look at
   regarde, ça ne vous ... **pas** it's none of your business
règle *f.* rule, ruler
régler to pay (a bill); to regulate
règne *m.* reign
regret *m.* regret
reine *f.* queen
rejoindre to joint, to meet
remarquer to notice
   faire ... to call one's attention to
   se faire ... to attract attention
remercier to thank
remettre to postpone, to put again
remonter to go up again
remplacer to replace
remplir to fill
rencontre *f.* meeting, encounter
   aller à la ... **de** to go to meet
rencontrer to meet
rendez-vous *m.* appointment, meeting-place, engagement

rendre to give back, to render
   se ... to betake oneself, to go
   se ... **compte** to realize
   se ... **dans un lieu** to betake oneself
renseignement *m.* information
renseigner, se inquire, to
rentrer to go back, to return
répandre to spread
réparer to repair
repas *m.* meal
repasser to iron
répertoire *m.* repertory
répéter to repeat
répondre to answer
repos *m.* rest
reposer to replace, to put again, to rest
   se ... to rest
représentant *m.* representative, agent
représenter to represent
représentation *f.* performance (of a play)
repriser to mend
répugner to be distasteful
réseau *m.* network
reservoir à essence *m.* gas tank
résidence *f.* residence
résoudre to resolve
   s ... to make up one's mind
respect *m.* respect
respirer to breathe
ressemblance *f.* resemblance
ressembler to resemble
ressort *m.* spring
restaurant *m.* restaurant
reste *m.* rest, remainder
rester to stay, to remain
restriction *f.* restriction
resumer to sum up
rétablir to reestablish
   se ... to regain one's health
retard *m.* delay
   en ... late
retarder to be slow, to delay
retenir to retain
retourner to return
   se ... to turn around

retrouver to find again,
   to meet
réussir to succeed
réveil *m.* alarm clock
réveiller to waken
   se ... to wake up
revenir to return, come back
revenu *m.* income
revoir to see again
   au ... good-bye, so long
rez-de-chaussée *f.* ground
   floor
rhume *m.* cold
   attraper un ... to catch cold
rideau,-x *m.* curtain
riche rich
rien nothing
rire to laugh
rive *f.* bank (of a river)
rivière *f.* river
robe *f.* dress
rognon *m.* kidney
roi *m.* king
rôle *m.* part (in a play)
roman *m.* novel
roman *adj.* romanesque
romancier *m.* novelist
romantique *m.* Romanticist
romantisme *m.* Romanticism
rompre to break
rond,-e round
rosbif *m.* roast beef
rose *f.* rose
rôti *m.* roast
rôti,-e roasted
rôtir to roast
roue *f.* wheel
rouge red
   ... à lèvres *m.* lipstick
rouler to roll, to run
route *f.* road, route
ruban *m.* ribbon
rubis *m.* ruby, jewel (watch)
rudement deucedly, harshly
rue *f.* street
ruine *f.* ruin
russe *m., f.* Russian
Russie *f.* Russia
rustique rustic

S

sable *m.* sand
sac *m.* bag
   ... à main handbag
saignant,-e raw
saigner to bleed
saisir to seize
saison *f.* season
salade *f.* salad
sale dirty
salé,-e salted
salir to dirty
salle *f.* hall, room
   ... à manger dining room
   ... de bain bathroom
   ... de théâtre playhouse,
   theater
   ... d'attente waiting room
   ... des bagages baggage
   room
salon *m.* living-room
salutation *f.* greeting
samedi *m.* Saturday
sandwich *m.* sandwich
sans without
   ... que without
santé *f.* constitution, health
satisfaire to satisfy
sauf except
sauter to jump
sauver to save
   se ... to go, to run along
savoir to know
savon *m.* soap
   ... à barbe *m.* shaving
   soap
sceau *m.* seal
scène *f.* stage, scene
second,-e second
seize sixteen
séjour *m.* sojourn, stay
sel *m.* salt
selon according to
semaine *f.* week
sembler to seem
semelle *f.* sole (of shoe)
sens unique *m.* one way street
sentiment *m.* sentiment
sentir to feel, to smell
   se ... to feel

sept seven
septembre *m.* September
sérieux,-euse serious
serré,-e tight
serrure *f.* lock
serviette *f.* napkin, towel
   ... hygiénique sanitary
     napkin
   ... de bain bath towel
service *m.* favor, service
   à votre ... at your service
servir to serve
   se ... de to use, to make
     use of
ses his, her
seul,-e alone
seulement only, solely
short *m.* shorts
siècle *m.* century
si yes, so, if
siège *m.* seat
signe *m.* sign
signer to sign
s'il vous plaît if you please
simplicité *f.* simplicity
simplement simply
sincère sincere
sincèrement sincerely
six six
ski, faire du to ski
ski *m.* ski
smoking *m.* tuxedo
soeur *f.* sister
soie *f.* silk
   ... artificielle *f.* artificial
     silk
soif *f.* thirst
soir *m.* evening
soirée *f.* evening party
soixante-dix seventy
soixante-quinze seventy-five
soldat *m.* soldier
soleil *m.* sun
   le lever du ... sunrise
   le coucher du ... sunset
sombre dark
somme *f.* sum
   en ... in short
somptueux,-euse sumptuous
son his, her, its
sonder to feel out

sonner to sound, ring
sonnette *f.* bell, buzzer
sorte *f.* kind, type
   de ... que so that
sortie *f.* exit
sortir to go out
souci *m.* worry
soudain sudden
souffle *m.* breath
souffrir to suffer
souhaiter to wish
soulier *m.* shoe
soupe *f.* soup
souper *m.* supper
souper to have supper
sourd,-e deaf
sourire *m.* smile
sous under
souscrire to subscribe
soutien *m.* support
soutien-gorge *m.* brassiere
souvenir remembrance
   se ... de to remember
souvent often
spectacle *m.* spectacle, show
spectateur *m.* spectator
sport *m.* sport
sportif,-ve sporting
subordonner to subordinate
subventionner to subsidize
succursale *f.* branch
   (of a firm)
sucre *m.* sugar
sucré,-e sweet
sucrier *m.* sugar bowl
sud *m.* south
suffire to suffice
Suisse *f.* Switzerland
suisse *adj.* Swiss
suite *f.* continuation, suite
   tout de ... immediately,
suivant,-e following
suivre to follow
   ... un cours to attend a
     course
sujet *m.* subject
supérieur,-e superior
supprimer to suppress
sur on
sûr, sûre sure

surhumain,-e superhuman
sur-le-champ on the spot, right
away; right there and then
sur mesure custom made
surprendre to surprise
surprise f. surprise
surtout above all, especially
surveiller to supervise,
to watch
sympathie f. sympathy
sympathique likable
symptôme m. symptom
syndicat m. syndicate,
union (of workers)
synonyme m. synonym
système m. system

T

tabac m. tobacco
bureau de ... tobacco store
table f. table
tableau m. picture, painting
tablier m. apron
tâcher to try
taille f. waist, stature
tailler to cut
tailleur m. tailor
costume ... woman's suit
talent m. talent
talon m. heel
tandis que whereas
tant so many, so much
... de so many, so much
... que as long as
tante f. aunt
tapis m. rug
tard late (in the day)
tarder to delay, to defer
... à to be late in, to delay,
to put off
... de to be anxious to
tarte f. pie
tas m. pile, lot
tasse f. cup
taux m. rate
... de change rate of
exchange
taxe f. tax
taxi m. taxi
teindre to dye
tel,-le such a

téléphone m. telephone
coup de ... telephone call
téléphoner to telephone
téléphoniste m., f. telephone
operator
tellement so, so much
témoin m. witness
tempête f. storm
temps m. time, weather,
à ... on time
de ... en ... once in a while
en même ... at the same
time
tendance f. tendency
tendancieux,-euse tendentious
tendre tender
tenir to hold
... à to be anxious to,
to be fond of
... compte to take into
account, to heed
... de to resemble, to take
after
tennis m. tennis
tenter to tempt
terminus m. terminal
terrasse f. terrace, sidewalk
café
tête f. head
avoir mal à la .... to have a
headache
thé m. tea
théâtre m. theater
thermomètre m. thermometer
tiens well!, indeed!
tiers m. third
timbre m. stamp
tirer to pull
se ... d'affaire to get along,
to manage
se bien ... de to come off
well
... d'un mauvais pas
to get out of a bad fix
tissu m. cloth
toile f. linen
toilette f. toilet
faire sa ... to get dressed
toit m. roof
tomate f. tomato
tombeau m. tomb

tomber to fall
torrent *m.* torrent
  à . . . s pouring
tort *m.* wrong
  avoir . . . to be wrong
torturer to torture
tôt soon, early
toucher to cash, to touch
toujours always, still
tour *f.* tower
tour *m.* tour, trip, turn
tourelle *f.* turret
tourne-vis *m.* screw-driver
tourner to turn
tournoi *m.* tournament
tout-e, tous, toutes all, every
  . . . à coup suddenly
  . . . à fait entirely
  . . . d'un coup suddenly
  . . . de même anyhow, just
  the same
toux *f.* cough
trac *m.* stage fright
trahir to betray
train *m.* train
  en . . . de in the act of
traire to milk
trait *m.* trait
traite *f.* draft (commercial)
traiter to treat
trajet *m.* trip
tramway *m.* trolley
tranche *f.* slice
transaction *f.* transaction
transatlantique transatlantic
  un train . . . a transatlantic
  boat train
transpiration *f.* perspiration
transporter to transport, carry
travail *m.* work
travailler to work
travers *m.* breadth
  à . . . across, through
traversée *f.* crossing
traverser *f.* cross
trempé,-e soaked
très very
trêve *f.* truce
  . . . de enough
triste sad
tristesse *f.* sadness

tromper to deceive
  se . . . to be wrong
trop too, too much
trottoir *m.* sidewalk
trouver to find
  se . . . to be (in a place)
tu you
tutelle *f.* tutelage
tutoyer to address familiarly,
  as **tu**

U

un,-e *m. f.,* a, an, one
uniformité *f.* uniformity
uniquement exclusively
université *f.* university
urgence *f.* urgency
us *m. pl.* usages
  . . . et coutumes ways and
  customs
usage *m.* use costum
usine *f.* factory, plant
utile useful
utiliser to use

V

vacances *f.pl.* vacation,
  cours de . . . summer session
vaisselle *f.* the dishes
vaguement vaguely
valable valuable
valeurs *f.* valuables, securities
valise *f.* suitcase, valise
vallée *f.* valley
valoir to be worth
  . . . mieux to be better
  (preferable)
  . . . la peine to be worth
  the trouble
vapeur *f.* steam
veau *m.* veal
véhicule *m.* vehicle
veine *f.* luck
  avoir de la . . . to be lucky
velours *m.* velvet
vendeuse *f.* saleslady
vendre to sell
vendredi *m.* Friday
venger to avenge
venir to come
  . . . de to have just

vente *f.* sale
vergogne *f.* shame
vérité *f.* truth
verre *m.* glass
vers about, toward
vert,-e green
vertige *m.* dizziness
veste *f.* jacket
vestiaire *m.* checkroom,
   cloakroom
veston *m.* sport coat
vêtement *m.* dress, garment,
   clothes
veuillez please
viande *f.* meat
   ... frigorifiée frozen meat
vie *f.* life, living
vieillesse *f.* old age
vieux, vieil, vieille old
vieux jeu old-fashioned
vif, vive alive
ville *f.* city, town
   en pleine ... in the center
   of the city
vin *m.* wine
vinaigre *m.* vinegar
vingt twenty
vingtaine *f.* about twenty
vis *f.* screw
visa *m.* visa
visage *m.* face
visière *f.* vizor
visite *f.* visit
   ... douanière *f.* customs
   examination
visiter to visit
visiteur *m.* visitor
vite quickly, fast

vitrail,-aux *m.* stained glass
   window
voici here is, here are
voie *f.* way, track
voilà there is; well!, there you
   are!
voir to see
voisin,-e *m. f.,* neighbor,
   neighboring
voiture *f.* automobile,
   carriage, railway car
voix *f.* voice
volant *m.* steering wheel
voler to fly, to steal
volontiers willingly
vos your
votre your
vôtre yours
vouloir to want
   ... bien to be willing
vous you
voyage *m.* trip
voyager to travel
voyageur,-euse *m.* traveler
vrai,-e true
vraiment truly, really
vue *f.* sight, view, eyesight

W X Z

wagon *m.* railroad car
wagon-lit *m.* sleeping-car
wagon-restaurant *m.* dining
   car
y there (place already
   mentioned)
y a-t-il? is there? are there?
zéro *m.* zero

ENGLISH-FRENCH DICTIONARY

A

a un, une
able, to be pouvoir
about à peu près
above au-dessus, dessus
absent absent,-e
absolutely absolument
absorbent cotton coton hydrophile m.
accelerator accélérateur m.
accept accepter
accent accent m.
accident accident m.
accompany accompagner
according to selon
account compte m.
accuse, to accuser
accustomed, to be habituer
acquaintance connaissance f.
across à travers
across the street en face
act, to agir
act acte m.
activity activité f.
address adresse f.
address, to adresser
address familiarly, to tutoyer
admire admirer
advice, conseil m.
afraid, to be avoir peur
after après
afternoon après-midi f.
afterwards ensuite
again de nouveau
against contre
age âge m.

agent représentant m.
agree, to être d'accord
agreeable agréable
airplane avion m.
air line route aérienne f.
airplane avion m.
airport aéroport m.
air mail par avion
air sickness mal d'avion m.
air valve soupape d'air f.
alarm clock réveil m.
alcohol alcool m.
alive vif, vive
all tout, tous
all aboard! en voiture!
almost presque
alone seul,-e
already déjà
also aussi
always toujours
America Amérique f.
American américain,-e
amiable aimable
among parmi, entre
amusing amusant,-e
and et
angry fâché,-e
announce annoncer
annoying ennuyeux,-euse
answer réponse f.
answer, to répondre
any aucun,-e
anyhow tout de même
apartment appartement m.
appear paraître
appearance air m.
appetite appétit m.

apple pomme *f.*
appointment rendez-vous *m.*
approach, to approcher
approximately à peu près
April avril *m.*
argue discuter
armchair fauteuil *m.*
arrange arranger
arrival arrivée *f.*
arrive arriver
art art *m.*
artificial artificiel,-le
as comme
as for quand à
as much autant
as soon as aussitôt que,
    dès que
as to quand à
ask, to demander
ask a question, to
    poser une question
asparagus asperge *f.*
aspirin aspirine *f.*
at chez, à
attach attacher
attack, to attaquer
August août *m.*
aunt tante *f.*
authentic authentique
author auteur *m.*
automatic automatique
automobile voiture *f.*
avenue avenue *f.*
average moyen,-ne
avoid éviter

B

bacon petit lard *m.*
bad mauvais,-e
badly mal
bag sac *m.*
baggage bagage *m.*
    ... check bulletin de
    bagage
baker boulanger *m.*
ball (dance) bal *m.*
banana banane *f.*
band-aid sparadrap *m.*
bandage bandage *m.*
bank banque *f.*

bank (of a river) rive *f.*
bar bar *m.*
barber coiffeur *m.*
bargain, to marchander
barometer baromètre *m.*
barrel tonneau *m.*
basin bassin *m.*
basket corbeille *f.*
bath bain *m.*
bathe se baigner
bathing suit
    costume de bain *m.*
bathroom salle de bain *f.*
bathtub baignoire *f.*
be, to être
beach plage *f.*
beach umbrella parasol *m.*
bean haricot *m.*
beard barbe *f.*
beautiful beau, bel, belle
beauty beauté *f.*
because parce que, à cause de
become, to devenir
bed lit *m.*
bedroom chambre à coucher *f.*
bedroom slippers pantoufles *f.*
bee abeille *f.*
beef boeuf *m.*
beer bière *f.*
before avant
beg, to prier
begin commencer
beginning commencement *m.*
beginning with à partir de
behavior conduite *f.*
behind derrière
Belgian belge
believe croire
bell sonnette *f.*
bell-boy groom *m.*
belong appartenir
berth couchette *f.*
best, the le meilleur
better *adv.* mieux
better *adj.* meilleur,-e
between entre
beware *interj.* gare
bicycle bicyclette *f.*
big grand,-e
bill addition *f.* (restaurant)
    facture (all else)

bill (cash) billet *m.*
bill-fold portefeuille *m.*
bird oiseau *m.*
birth naissance *f.*
birthday anniversaire *m.*
bite, to mordre
bitter amer,-ère
black noir,-e
blade lame *f.*
blanket couverture *f.*
bleach, to décolorer
bleed saigner
blouse blouse *f.*
blow coup *m.*
blow out, to crever
blue bleu,-e
blunder gaffe *f.*
boarding-house pension *f.*
boat bateau *m.*
body corps *m.*
boiled bouilli,-e
bolt boulon *m.*
bone os *m.*
book livre *m.*
bookstore librairie *f.*
border frontière *f.*
border, to border
bored, to be s'ennuyer
boric acid acide borique *m.*
boring ennuyeux
boss patron *m.*
bother, to ennuyer
bottle bouteille *f.*
bottom fond *m.*
box boîte *f.*
box office guichet *m.*
boy garçon *m.*
bracelet bracelet *m.*
brake frein *m.*
branch (of tree) branche *f.*
branch (of a firm) succursale *f.*
brand marque *f.*
brandy cognac *m.*
brassiere soutien-gorge *m.*
breakfast petit déjeuner *m.*
bread pain *m.*
breadth travers *m.*
break, to casser
breakdown (of an automobile)
  panne *f.*
breath souffle *m.*

breathe respirer
bridge pont *m.*
bring apporter
bring back ramener
  rapporter
broken (out of order)
  détraqué,-e
brother frère *m.*
brush brosse *f.*
build to construire
building bâtiment, édifice *m.*
bus autobus *m.*
business affaires *f.pl.*
business commercial,-e
business firm
  maison de commerce *f.*
busy occupé,-e
but mais
butter beurre *m.*
button bouton *m.*
buy, to acheter
buzzer sonnette *f.*
by par

C

cabaret cabaret *m.*
cabbage chou *m.*
cabin cabine *f.*
cablegram câble *m.*
cake gâteau,-x *m.*
call appeler
campaign campagne *f.*
cancel, to annuler
cap casquette *f.*
capital capital *m.*
car auto *f.*
car door portière *f.*
carbon carbone *m.*
carburetor carburateur *m.*
card carte *f.*
carpenter menuisier *m.*
carrot carotte *f.*
carry porter
carry off emporter
case cas *m.*
cash a check encaisser un
  chèque
castle château,-x *m.*
cat chat *m.*

catch attraper
cathedral cathédrale f.
cauliflower chou-fleur m.
cause cause f.
cave grotte f.
caviar caviar m.
ceiling plafond m.
celebrate, to célébrer
cellar cave f.
cement ciment m.
center centre m.
central heating chauffage
    central m.
century siècle m.
cereals céréales f. pl.
certainly certainement
chair chaise f.
chalk craie f.
chambermaid femme de
    chambre f.
change monnaie f.
change, to changer
change purse porte-monnaie
    m.
chapel chapelle f.
chapter chapitre m.
character caractère,
    personnage m.
characteristic caractéristique
charm charme m.
charmed enchanté,-e
charming charmant,-e
cheap bon marché
cheaper moins cher
check chèque m.
check, to contrôler, voir
checkroom consigne f.
    vestiaire m.
cheese fromage m.
chef chef m.
chest poitrine f., coffre m.
chestnut marron m.
chew, to mâcher
chief chef m.
child enfant m. f.
chin menton m.
chocolate chocolat m.
choice choix m.
choose choisir
chop côtelette f.
church église f.

cigar cigarre m.
cigarette cigarette f.
city ville f.
city hall hôtel de ville m.
claim, to prétendre
clarity clarté f.
class classe f.
classical classique
climate climat m.
clean, to nettoyer
clean propre
clear clair,-e, net,-te
clear the table desservir
climb monter
clinic clinique f.
cloakroom vestiaire m.
clock horloge f.
close, to fermer
close fitting ajusté,-e
closing fermeture f.
cloth étoffe, tissue, toile f.
clothes vêtements f. pl.
    toile f.
clothing habillement m.
cloud nuage m.
coat manteau m.
coffee café m.
cold froid,-e
cold (head) rhume m.
collar col m.
color couleur f.
column colonne f.
comb peigne m.
comb (hair) coiffer
    (les cheveux)
come venir
comedy comédie f.
comfort confort m.
comfortable confortable
commerce commerce m.
commonly communément
communicate, to
    communiquer
communication
    communication f.
company compagnie f.
compare, to comparer
comparison comparaison f.
compartment compartiment
    m.

complete complet,-ète
completely complètement
complicated compliqué,-e
compliment compliment *m.*
concert concert *m.*
conclude to conclure
condition état *f.*
congratulation félicitation *f.*
conservatory conservatoire *m.*
consider, to considérer
consist, to consister
constantly constamment
consulate consulat *m.*
consult, to consulter
consultation consultation *f.*
continental continental,-aux
continuation suite *f.*
continue, to continuer
contract contrat *m.*
contradict contredire
contrary contraire *m.*
contrast contraste *m.*
convenient convenable
conversation conversation *f.*
converse, to causer
cook cuisinier,-ère *m.,f.*
cook, to cuire
cooked cuit,-e
cool frais, fraîche
copy copie *f.*
copy (duplicate) exemplaire
    m.
cordially cordialement
cork liège *m.*
corner coin *m.*
correct, to corriger
corridor corridor, *m.*
cost prix *m.*
cost, to coûter
cotton coton *m.*
cough toux *f.*
count compter
countless innombrable
country campagne *f.*
    pays *m.*
course (in school) cours *m.*
course plat *m.*
court house palais de justice
    m.
courtier courtisan *m.*
courtyard cour *f.*

cousin cousin *m., f.*
cover couvert *m.*
cover, to couvrir
cow vache *f.*
cray-fish langouste *f.*
crazy fou, folle
cream crème *f.*
create, to créer
credit crédit *m.*
crisis crise *f.*
critical critique
cross croix *f.*
cross, to traverser
crossing traversée *f.*
crowd foule *f.*
crumb miette *f.*
cuff manchette *f.*
cuff link bouton de manchette
    m.
cup tasse *f.*
cure, to guérir
curl boucle *f.*
currency monnaie *f.*
current courant
curtain rideau *m.*
custom coutume *f.*
custom-house douane *f.*
custom made sur mesure
customer client *m.*
customs douane
customs examination
    visite douanière *f.*
customs officer douanier *m.*
cut, to couper, tailler
cutlet côtelette *f.*
cylinder cylindre *m.*

D

dainty coquet,-te
damage dommage *m.*
damn, to damner
damp humide
dance, to danser
danger danger *m.*
dangerous dangereux,-euse
dare, to oser
dark sombre, foncé,-e
darkness obscurité *f.*
darling chéri,-e
date date *f.*
daughter fille *f.*

dawn aube *f.*
day jour *m.* journée *f.*
dead mort,-e
deaf sourd,-e
dear cher, chère
death mort *f.*
debt dette *f.*
decanter carafe *f.*
deceive, to tromper
December décembre *m.*
deck-chair chaise-longue *f.*
declare déclarer
decorate décorer
deed fait *m.*
defend défendre
degree degré, grade *m.*
delay retard *m.*
delay, to retarder
delicacy délicatesse *f.*
delicate délicat,-e
delicious delicieux,-euse
deliver livrer
delivery livraison *f.*
demolish, to démolir
dentist dentiste *m.*
depart, to partir
departmental capital
  préfecture *f.*
departure départ *m.*
depend, to dépendre
deposit, to déposer
desire, to désirer
desk bureau *m.*
dessert dessert *m.*
destination destination *f.*
detailed détaillé,-e
detective policier *m.*
detest, to détester
develop, to développer
devote, to consacrer
diamond diamant *m.*
dictionary dictionnaire *m.*
die, to mourir
difference différence *f.*
difference, make no be égal
different différent,-e, divers,-e
difficult difficile
difficulty difficulté *f.*
digestion digestion *f.*
dine, to dîner

dining-car wagon-restaurant *m.*
dining-room salle à manger *f.*
dinner dîner *m.*
diploma diplôme *m.*
direct direct,-e
directly directement
dirty, to salir
dirty sale
disappear, to disparaître
discover, to découvrir
discuss, to discuter
disembark débarquer
disgust repulsion *f.*
dish plat *m.*
dishes vaisselle *f.*
distance distance *f.*
distant lointain,-e
distinguished distingué,-e
disturb déranger
dive, to plonger
divide diviser
dizziness vertige *m.*
do, to faire
dock quai *m.*
doctor médecin *m.* docteur *m.*
door porte *f.*
double double
double to doubler
double bed lit à deux places *m.*
doubt doute *m.*
doubt, to douter
down à bas
dozen douzaine *f.*
draft courant d'air *m.*
draft (commercial) traite *f.*
dramatist dramaturge *m.*
draw closer, to se rapprocher
dress robe *f.*
dress, to habiller
dressmaker couturier *m.*
dressed, to get faire sa toilette, s'habiller
dresser commode *f.*
dressing gown robe de chambre *f.*
drink, to boire
drink boisson *f.*
drive, to conduire

driver chauffeur, conducteur *m.*
driver's license permis de conduire *m.*
drugstore pharmacie *f.*
druggist pharmacien *m.*
dry clean, to faire nettoyer à sec
duck canard *m.*
during pendant
duty devoir *m.*
dwell, to habiter
dye, to faire teindre

E

each chacun,-e, chaque
ear oreille *f.*
early tôt
earn gagner
earring boucle d'oreille *f.*
easily facilement
east est *m.*
easy facile
eat manger
edge bord *m.*
effect effet *m.*
egg oeuf *m.*
  soft-boiled . . .oeuf à la coque
  fried . . . oeuf sur le plat
eight huit
eighteen dix-huit
eighth huitième
elbow coude *m.*
elect élire
electric électrique
electricity électricité *f.*
elegant élégant,-e, chic
elevator ascenceur *m.*
eleven onze
elsewhere ailleurs
embark s'embarquer
embroider, to broder
employee employé,-e *m.,f.*
empty vide
end bout *m.*, fin *f.*
engine moteur *m.*
engineer ingénieur *m.*
England Angleterre *f.*
English anglais,-e

enjoy jouir de
enormous énorme
enormously énormément
enough assez
enter, to entrer
enthusiasm enthousiasme *m.*
entire entier,-ère
entirely entièrement
entrance entrée *f.*
envelope enveloppe *f.*
epoch époque *f.*
equal égal,-e
equipment matériel *m.*
eraser gomme *f.*
error erreur *f.*
especially surtout
establish établir
evening soir *m.*
  soirée *f.*
event événement *m.*
everybody tout le monde
everywhere partout
exact exact,-e, exactement
exactly au juste
examination examen *m.*
examine examiner
example exemple *m.*
  for . . . par exemple
excellent excellent,-e
except sauf,excepté
exception exception *f.*
exercise excercice *m.*
excess luggage bagage en excédent *m.*
exchange échange *m.*
exchange, to échanger
exciting passionant,-e
exclusively uniquement
excursion excursion *f.*
excuse excuser
excuse me pardonnez-moi
exit sortie *f.*
expensive cher, chère
experience expérience *f.*
experience, to éprouver
experienced expérimenté
explain expliquer
explanation explication *f.*
export, to exporter
express, to exprimer
expression expression *f.*

extinguish éteindre
extraordinary extraordinaire
extreme extrême
eye oeil *m.*
eye glasses lunettes *f.*
eyesight vue *f.*

F

face figure *f.*, visage *m.*
face massage massage facial
factory usine *f.*
faint, to s'évanouir
fall, to tomber
Fall automne *f.*
false faux, fausse
family famille *f.*
famous célèbre, fameux,-euse,
    illustre
far loin
fare prix du billet *m.*
fashion mode *f.*
fast vite, rapide
fat gros,-se
fat gras *m.*
father père *m.*
favor service *m.*
favorable favorable
favorite favori,-ite
fear peur *f.*
fear, to craindre
February février *m.*
fee honoraires *m., pl.*
feel, to se sentir, sentir
feel out, to sonder
feel sick, to avoir mal au coeur
felt hat feutre *m.*
fertilizer engrais *m.*
festival fête *f.*
fever fièvre *f.*
fifteen quinze
fifth cinquième
fifty cinquante
fill, to remplir
fillet filet *m.*
film rouleau *m.*
film negative pellicule *f.*
filter filtre *m.*
finally enfin
find trouver
find again retrouver

find out (about) se renseigner
finger doigt *m.*
finger nail ongle *m.*
finish finir
fire feu *m.*
first premier,-ère
first (at) d'abord
fish poisson *m.*
fish, to pêcher
fishing pêche *f.*
five cinq
flannel flanelle *f.*
flat plat,-e
flatter, to flatter
flight vol *m.*
float, to flotter
floor étage *m.*, plancher *m.*
floor, first rez-de-chaussée *m.*
florist fleuriste *m., f.*
flower fleur *f.*
fluently couramment
fly mouche *f.*
fly, to voler
foggy brumeux,-euse
fortress château fort *m.*
fold pli *m.*
follow suivre
following suivant,-e
fond of, to be tenir à
foot pied *m.*
football football *m.*
for car, pour
forbid défendre
forbidden interdit,-e
force, to forcer
foreign etranger,-ère
foreigner étranger,-ère *m., f.*
fork fourchette *f.*
forget oublier
form, to former
form forme *f.*
formality formalité *f.*
formerly autrefois
formula formule *f.*
fortress château fort *m.*
fortunately heureusement
fountain fontaine *f.*
fountain pen stylo *m.*
four quatre
fourteen quatorze

fourth quatrième
frame cadre *m.*
franc franc *m.* (money)
France France *f.*
free libre
freedom liberté *f.*
freeze, to geler
French français,-e
fresh frais, fraîche
Friday vendredi *m.*
friend ami,-e *m., f.*
frighten faire peur à
frost gelée *f.*
fruit fruit *m.*
fry, to frire
function, to fonctionner
funds fonds *m.pl.*
funny drôle
fur fourrure, *f.*
furnish fournir, meubler
furnished room chambre
  meublée *f.*
furniture (piece of) meuble *m.*

G

gallery galerie *f.*
game jeu *m.*
gang plank passerelle *f.*
garage garage *m.*
garage man dépanneur *m.*
garden jardin *m.*
garlic ail *m.*
garment vêtement *m.*
garters jarretières *f.*
gas gaz *m.*
gasoline essence *f.*
gas tank reservoir à essence
  m.
gastronomy gastronomie *f.*
gate barrière *f.*
gauze bandage
  gaze hydrophile *f.*
gay gai,-e
general général,-e
general delivery poste
  restante *f.*
generally généralement
gentlemen messieurs
geometric géométrique
get up, to se lever

gift cadeau *m.*
girdle gaine *f.*
girl jeune fille *f.*
give, to donner
give back rendre
glass verre *m.*
glory gloire *f.*
glove gant *m.*
go aller
go down, to descendre
go out, to sortir
go up, to monter
goat chèvre *f.*
God Dieu
gold or *m.*
golf golf *m.*
good bon,-ne
good-bye au revoir
good day bonjour
good evening bonsoir
good luck bonne chance
good morning bonjour
government gouvernement
  m.
graceful gracieux,-euse
grape raisin *m.*
grapefruit pamplemousse *m.*
grateful reconnaissant,-e
grass herbe *f.*
gravy jus *m.*
great grand,-e
Greek grec,-que
green vert,-e
greeting salutation *f.*
grocery store épicerie *f.*
grow, to croître, pousser,
  grandir
guarantee to garantir
guardian gardien *m.*
guest invité *m.* or *f.*
guide, to guider
guide guide *m.*

H

habit coutume *f.*
haircut coupe *f.*
hairdresser coiffeur *m.*
half demi,-e, moitié *f.*
hail, to héler
hall porter garçon *m.*

halt halte f.
ham jambon m.
hamlet hameau m.
hand main f.
handbag sac à main m.
handkerchief mouchoir m.
handlebar guidon m.
hang up raccrocher
happy content,-e, heureux,
   -euse
harbor port m.
hard dur,-e
harmful, to be nuire à
harmonious harmonieux,-euse
harshly rudement
hat chapeau,-x m.
have, to avoir
have to, to devoir, falloir
he il
head tête f.
headache mal à la tête m.
health santé f.
healthy sain,-e
hear entendre
heart coeur m.
hearth foyer m.
heat chaleur f.
heat, to chauffer
heating chauffage m.
heavy lourd
heel talon m.
height hauteur f.
hell enfer m.
hello bonjour
help, to aider
helping portion f.
her elle, son, sa
here ici
here is, are voici
hesitate, to hésiter
hide, to cacher
high haut,-e, élevé,-e
high school collège m.,
   lycée m.
hill côte f.
hire, to louer
historical historique
history histoire f.
hit, to frapper
hitchhike, to faire de l'auto-
   stop

hold, to tenir
holiday jour de congé m.
holidays vacances f.
home domicile m.
honey miel m.
honeymoon lune de miel f.
honor, to honorer
honor honneur m.
hope, to espérer
horse cheval,-aux m.
horse-cab fiacre m.
hospital hôpital m.
hot chaud,-e
hotel hôtel m.
hour heure f.
house maison f.
how comment
how many combien
how much combien
however cependant, pourtant
human humain,-e
humidity humidité f.
humor humour m.
hundred cent m.
hunger faim f.
hungry, to be avoir faim
hungry affamé,-e
hunting chasse f.
hurry, to se dépêcher
hurt, to faire mal
husband mari m.

I

I je
ice glace f.
ice-cream glace f.
idea idée f.
identification card carte
   d'identité f.
identification paper pièce
   d'identité f.
identify, to identifier
identity identité f.
if si
ignition allumage m.
imagine, to se figurer,
   imaginer
immediate immédiat,-e
immediately tout de suite
   immédiatement
impatient impatient,-e

import importation *f.*
import, to importer
importance importance *f.*
impress impressioner
impression impression *f.*
impressive impressionant,-e
improve, to se perfectionner
in dans, en
in front of devant
in order to pour
income revenu *m.*
income tax impôt sur le
   revenu *m.*
inconvenience, to déranger
increase augmenter
indicate, to indiquer
indirect indirect,-e
indirectly indirectement
individual individuel,-le
inferior inférieur
infinite infini,-e
infinitely infiniment
inform aviser
information renseignement *m.*
   information *f.*
informed, to be être au courant de
inhabitant habitant *m.*
ink encre *f.*
inquire, to se renseigner
inscribe inscrire
insect repellent insecticide *m.*
inside dedans
insist, to insister
institute institut *m.*
insult injure *f.*
insurance assurance *f.*
intellectual intellectuel,-le
intelligence intelligence *f.*
intention intention *f.*
interest intérêt *m.*
interesting intéressant,-e
interior intérieur,-e
intermission entr'acte *m.*
interpreter interprète *m.*
intrepid intrépide
introduction introduction *f.*
intruder intrus *m.*
invitation invitation *f.*
invite inviter
invited invité,-e

iodine iode *m.*
iron fer *m.*
iron, to repasser
ironical ironique
island île *f.*
it il, elle
Italian italien,-ne
itinerary itinéraire *m.*

J

jack cric *m.*
jacket veste, jaquette *f.*
jam confiture *f.*
janitor concierge *m., f.*
January janvier *m.*
jewel bijou,-x *m.*
jeweler bijoutier *m.*
join joindre
joke plaisanterie *f.*
joke, to plaisanter
journal (personal) agenda *m.*
joy joie *f.*
July juillet *m.*
jump sauter
June juin *m.*
justice justice *f.*

K

keep garder
key clef *f.*
kidney rognon *m.*
kill, to tuer
kilogram kilo *m.*
kilometer kilomètre *m.*
kind gentil,-le
kind sorte, espèce *f.,*
   genre *m.*
kindness bienveillance *f.*
king roi *m.*
kiss, to embrasser
kitchen cuisine *f.*
knee genou *m.*
knife couteau *m.*
knock cogner, frapper
knot noeud *m.*
know connaître, savoir
knowledge connaissance *f.*
known connu,-e

L

labor main d'oeuvre *f.*
lace dentelle *f.*
lace, shoe lacet *m.*
lack, to manquer de
ladder échelle *f.*
ladies mesdames *f.*
lady dame *f.*
lake lac *m.*
lamb agneau *m.*
lamp lampe *f.*
lamp bulb ampoule *f.*
land, to débarquer
land (an airplane) atterrir
language langue *f.*
large grand,-e
last, dernier,-ère
last, to durer
late tard,-e
laugh rire
laundry blanchisserie *f.*
law loi *f.*
laziness paresse *f.*
lazy paressuex,-euse
lead, to mener
leaf feuille *f.*
learn apprendre
lease bail *m.*
least moindre
leather cuir *m.*
leave quitter, laísser
lecture conférence *f.*
left gauche *f.*
leg (meat) cuisse *f.*
leg (limb) jambe *f.*
lemon citron *m.*
lemonade limonade *f.*
lend, to prêter
lengthen allonger
less moins
lesson leçon *f.*
let, to laisser
letter lettre *f.*
letter of credit lettre de crédit *f.*
lettuce laitue *f.*
liaison liaison *f.*
library bibliothèque *f.*
lie mensonge *m.*
life vie *f.*

light clair,-e
light lumière *f.*
light, to allumer
light up, to éclairer
lighter briquet *m.*
lightning éclairs *m.pl.*
likable sympathique
like, to aimer
like comme
line ligne *f.*
linen toile *f.*
lip lèvre *f.*
lipstick rouge à lèvres *m.*
liqueur liqueur *f.*
listen écouter
literary littéraire
literature littérature *f.*
little petit,-e, peu
live demeurer, habiter
liver foie *m.*
living room salon *m.*
loaf miche *f.*
lobster homard *m.*
lock serrure *f.*
lodge, to loger
long long,-ue
long distance call interurbain
long time longtemps
look at regarder
look for chercher
look like, to avoir l'air de . . .
lose, to perdre
lost perdu,-e
lot tas *m.*
lounge foyer *m.*
love, to aimer
low bas,-se
luck chance, veine *f.* (slang)
lucky, to be avoir de la veine
lunch, to déjeuner
lunch déjeuner *m.*
lung poumon *m.*

M

machine machine *f.*
magic magique *adj.*
magnificent magnifique
maid bonne *f.*
mail courrier *m.*
main principal,-e

majesty majesté *f.*
majority plupart *f.*
make faire
man homme *m.*
manage, to se tirer d'affaire
  se débrouiller
management direction *f.*
manager directeur,-trice,
  gérant,-e
manicurist manicure *m.*
manner façon *f.*
manufacture, to fabriquer
manufacturing fabrication *f.*
map plan *m.*
March mars *m.*
mark marque *f.*
market marché *m.*
marriage, wedding mariage *m.*
marvellous merveilleux-euse
mashed potato purée de
  pomme de terre *f.*
match allumette *f.*
mattress matelas *m.*
May mai *m.*
me moi
meal repas *m.*
mean, to vouloir dire
measure mesure *f.*
meat viande *f.*
medicine médicament *m.*
meet rencontrer
meeting assemblée, rencontre
  f.
melon melon *m.*
member membre *m.*
memory mémoire *f.*
mend, to repriser
menu menu *m.*
merchant marchand *m.*
merchandise marchandise *f.*
message message *m.*
metal métal *m.*
meter compteur *m.*
middle milieu *m.*
midnight minuit *m.*
milliner modiste *f.*
milk lait *m.*
milk, to traire
mind esprit *m.*
mine mien, mienne
mineral water eau minérale *f.*

minute minute *f.*
mirror glace *f.*, miroir *m.*
misfortune malheur *m.*
mislay égarer
Miss mademoiselle
miss, to manquer
mistake erreur *m.*, faute *f.*
mister monsieur *m.*
misunderstanding malentendu
  m.
mix, to mélanger
mixture mélange *m.*
mob foule *f.*
mock moquer
modern moderne
moistness moiteur *f.*
moment moment, instant *m.*
Monday lundi *m.*
money argent *m.*
money order mandat-poste *m.*
monkey wrench clef anglaise *f.*
month mois *m.*
monument monument *m.*
moon lune *f.*
more plus, davantage
moreover puis, d'ailleurs
morning matin *m.*, matinée *f.*
mosquito moustique *m.*
most plupart
mother maman, mère *f.*
motor moteur *m.*
mountain montagne *f.*
moustache moustache *f.*
mouth bouche *f.*
move, to déplacer
move away, to déménager
move in s'installer
movement mouvement *m.*
movie camera appareil ciné-
  matographique *m.*
movie theatre cinéma *m.*
moving picture film *m.*
Mr. Monsieur, M.
Mrs. Madame, Mme
much beaucoup
museum musée *m.*
music musique *f.*
music hall music hall *m.*
musician musicien,-ne
mustard moutarde *f.*

n.y mon, ma, mes
mysterious mystérieux,-ieuse

N

nail clou, ongle (finger) *m.*
name nom *m.*
napkin serviette *f.*
narrow étroit,-e
natural naturel,-le
naturally naturellement
nature nature *f.*
nave nef *f.*
near près
nearly presque
necessary nécessaire
neck cou *m.*
necktie cravate *f.*
need, to avoir besoin de
needle aiguille *f.*
neighbor voisine,-e *m.*
neighborhood alentours *m. pl.*
neither ni, non plus
   . . . nor, ni . . . ni
nephew neveu *m.*
network réseau *m.*
never jamais
nevertheless pourtant,
   néanmoins
new neuf,-ve, nouveau,
   nouvel,-le
news nouvelles *f. pl.*
newspaper journal,-aux *m.*
newsstand kiosque *m.*
next prochain-e
next day lendemain *m.*
night nuit *f.*
night club boîte de nuit *f.*
nightgown chemise de nuit *f.*
nine neuf
nineteen dix-neuf
no admittance! defense
   d'entrer!
no trespassing accès interdit
noise bruit *m.*
no non
nobility noblesse *f.*
noise bruit *m.*
noon midi *m.*
north nord *m.*
not pas, ne . . . pas

not . . . anything ne . . . rien
notably notamment
notary notaire *m.*
notebook cahier *m.*
nothing rien
notice avis *m.*
notice, to remarquer
novel roman *m.*
November novembre *m.*
now maintenant
nowadays actuellement
number numéro *m.*
nurse infirmière *f.*
nut noix *f.*

O

obelisk obélisque *m.*
object objet *m.*
objective objectif,-ive
oblige obliger
observation observation *f.*
observe, to constater
obtain obtenir
obviously evidemment
occupant occupant *m.*
occupation occupation *f.*
occupy occuper
octagonal octogonal
October octobre *m.*
odor odeur *f.*
of de
of course bien entendu
offend, to offenser, froisser
offer, to offrir
offer offre *m.*
office bureau *m.*
official officiel,-le
often souvent
oil huile *f.*
ointment pommade *f.*
O.K. d'accord
old vieux, vieille, ancien,-ne
old age vieillesse *f.*
old-fashioned vieux jeu,
   suranné,-e
omelet omelette *f.*
on sur, dessus
once une fois
one un,-e
one way street sens unique *m.*

onion *m.* oignon
only seulement
open ouvert,-e
open, to ouvrir
opera opéra *m.*
opinion opinion *f.*, avis *m.*
oppose, to opposer
or ou
orange orange *f.*
order ordre *m.*
order, to commander
organize organiser
originality originalité *f.*
other autre
otherwise autrement
our notre, nos
ourselves nous-mêmes
outside dehors
over there là bas
over dessus, sur
overcoat pardessus *m.*
overseas outre-mer
overturn capotage *m.*
owe, to devoir
oysters huîtres *f.*

P

pack, to emballer
package paquet *m.*
page page *f.*
pain peine, douleur *f.*, mal *m.*
paint, to peindre
painting peinture *f.*,
    tableau *m.*
pair paire *f.*
palace palais *m.*
palate palais *m.*
pale pâle
palm (of hand) paume *f.*
panties culotte *f.*
paper papier *m.*
parcel colis *m.*
parcel post colis postal *m.*
pardon, to pardonner
pardon pardon *m.*
parent parent,-e *m., f.*
Parisian parisien,-ne
park the car garer la voiture
part part, partie *f.*

participate participer
pass, to passer
passport passeport *m.*
pastry pâtisserie *f.*
pastrymaker pâtissier,-ère
patriot patriote *m.*
pattern patron *m.*
pavillon kiosque *m.*
pay payer, régler
pay cash payer au comptant
payment paiement *m.*
peace paix *f.*
peach pêche *f.*
peanut cacahuète *f.*
pear poire *f.*
peas petits pois *m.*
pedal pédale *f.*
pedestrian piéton *m.*
peer pair *m.*
pen plume *f.*
pencil crayon *m.*
people monde, gens *m.*
pepper poivre *m.*
per par
perceive apercevoir
per cent pour cent
perfect parfait,-e
perfectly parfaitement
performance représentation *f.*
perfume parfum *m.*
perhaps peut-être
perish, to périr
permanent wave permanente
    f.
permit, to permettre
person personne *f.*
personal personnel,-le
perspiration transpiration *f.*
persuade persuader
petroleum pétrole *m.*
petticoat jupon *m.*
pharmacy pharmacie *f.*
photograph photo *f.*
physician médecin *m.*
piano piano *m.*
picture tableau *m.*
picture postcard carte postale
    illustrée *f.*
picturesque pittoresque
pie tarte *f.*
piece morceau *m.*

pier quai *m.*
pile tas *m.*
pill pilule *f.*
pillow oreiller, coussin *m.*
pilot pilote *m.*
pin épingle *f.*
pineapple ananas *m.*
pipe pipe *f.*
pity, to plaindre, avoir
    pitié de
place endroit, lieu *m.*
place, to placer, mettre
plan projet *m.*
plant plante *f.*
plate assiette *f.*
platform plate-forme *f.*
    quai *m.*
play pièce *f.*
play, to jouer
player joueur *m.*
playhouse salle de théâtre *f.*
pleasant aimable
please veuillez, s'il vous plaît
please, to plaire à
pleasure plaisir *m.*
plum prune *f.*
pocket poche *f.*
poem poème *m.*
poet poète *m.*
poetic poétique
poetry poésie *f.*
point point *m.*
police headquarters préfecture
    de police *f.*
police station commissariat *m.*
policeman gendarme, agent
    (de police) *m.*
polite poli
political politique
politics politique *f.*
poor pauvre
pork porc *m.*
port port *m.*
porter porteur *m.*
position position *f.*
possess, to posséder
possible possible
postage affranchissement *m.*
postman facteur *m.*
post office poste *f.*
postpone remettre

potato pomme de terre *f.*
pound livre *f.*
poverty misère *f.*
powder poudre *f.*
powder, to poudrer
practical commode, pratique
practice, to s'exercer
praise, to louer
pray prier
precise précis,-e
precisely justement
prefer préférer
prejudice préjugé *m.*
prepare préparer
prescription ordonnance *f.*
present actuel,-le
present, to présenter
press, to appuyer
presumptuous présomptueux,
    -euse
pretend, to prétendre
pretty poli,-e
prevent empêcher
previously auparavant
price prix *m.*
principal principal
print épreuve *f.*
private particulier,-ère,
    privé,-e
prize prix *m.*
probably probablement
procure procurer
produce, to produire
product produit *m.*
professional professionel,-le
profitable profitable
profound profond-e
program programme *m.*
promenade promenade *f.*
promise, to promettre
properly proprement
propose, to proposer
proscribe, to proscrire
protest protestation *f.*
prove prouver
pull, to tirer
pulse pouls *m.*
pump pompe *f.*
punctual ponctuel,-le
puncture crevaison *f.*

purchase, to acheter
purchase achat *m.*
pure pur,-e
purpose intention *f.*
purpose, on exprès
pursue, to poursuiure
push, to pousser
put placer, mettre
pyjamas pyjamas *m.*

Q

quality qualité *f.*
quarter quart *m.*
queen reine *f.*
question question *f.*
quickly vite
quit quitter
quote, to citer

R

rabbit lapin *m.*
race course *f.*
radiator radiateur *m.*
radio radio *f.*
radio station poste *m.*
railroad chemin de fer *m.*
railroad-car wagon *m.*
   voiture *f.*
railroad station gare *f.*
rain pluie *f.*
rain, to pleuvoir
raincoat imperméable *m.*
raise lever
rank rang *m.*
rate taux *m.*
rate of exchange taux de
   change
rather plutôt
raw saignant,-e
rayon rayonne *f.*
razor rasoir *m.*
razor blade lame à rasoir *f.*
reach, to parvenir
react réagir
read lire
reading lecture *f.*
ready prêt,-e
real réel,-le
realistic réaliste
really réellement, vraiment

rear arrière
reason, to raisonner
reason raison *f.*
reasonable raisonnable
reassure, to rassurer
recall, to rappeler
receipt reçu *m.*
receive recevoir
recently récemment
reception réception *f.*
recognize reconnaître
recommend recommander
recover récupérer
red rouge
reduce réduire
refresh, to rafraîchir
refreshment rafraîchissement
   m.
refrigerator frigidaire *m.*
refuse refuser
register se faire inscrire,
   enregistrer
register a letter faire recommander une lettre
registered letter lettre recommandée *f.*
regret regret *m.*
regret, to regretter
reign règne *m.*
relate raconter
relation relation *f.*
relative parent,-e
relish hors d'oeuvre *m.*
remake refaire
remain rester
remember se souvenir de
rent loyer *m.*
rent, to louer
repair réparer
repeat répéter
replace remplacer
represent représenter
resemblance ressemblance *f.*
resemble, to ressembler
reside demeurer
residence résidence *f.*
resolve résoudre
respect respect *m.*
rest (remainder) reste *m.*
rest repos *m.*
restaurant restaurant *m*

restriction restriction *f.*
retain retenir
return retourner, rentrer, revenir
ribbon ruban *m.*
rice riz *m.*
rich riche
ride promenade en voiture *f.*
right droit,-e
right away tout de suite
ring, to sonner
ring bague *f.* (on finger)
rise hausse *f.* (in prices)
river fleuve *m.*
road route *f.,* chemin *m.*
roast rôti *m.*
roast, to rôtir
roast beef rosbif *m.*
roasted rôti,-e
roll petit pain *m.*
roll, to rouler
roof toit *m.*
room chambre, pièce, salle *f.*
rose rose *f.*
rough rude
round rond,-e
row rang *m.*
rubber caoutchouc *m.*
ruby rubis *m.*
rug tapis *m.*
ruin ruine *f.*
ruler règle *f.*
run courir
run along, to se sauver
runner coureur *m.*
running water eau courante *f.*
rush hour heure d'affluence *f.*
Russia Russie *f.*
Russian russe
rustic rustique

S

sad triste
sadness tristesse *f.*
safe sauf, sauve
sail, to s'embarquer
salad salade *f.*
sale vente *f.*
saleslady vendeuse *f.*
salesman vendeur *m.*

salmon saumon *m.*
salt sel *m.*
salted salé,-e
same même
sand sable *m.*
sandwich sandwich *m.*
sanitary napkin, serviette hygiénique *f.*
satisfy, to contenter, satisfaire
Saturday samedi *m.*
save sauver
say, to dire
scarcely à peine
scene scène *f.*
scenery paysage *m.*
school école *f.*
scissors ciseaux *m.*
scrape, to gratter
scratch égratignure *f.*
scratch, to gratter
screw-driver tourne-vis *m.*
sea mer *f.*
seal sceau *m.*
season saison *f.*
seasickness mal de mer *m.*
seasoning assaisonnement *m.*
seat place *f.,* siège *m.*
second (time) seconde *f.*
second second,-e, deuxième
section of a city quartier *m.*
securities valeurs *f. pl.*
see voir
see again revoir
seem, to sembler
seize saisir
sell vendre
send envoyer
   . . . for envoyer chercher
sentence phrase *f.*
sentiment sentiment *m.*
September septembre *m.*
serious sérieux,-euse
seriously pour de bon
servant domestique *m., f.*
serve servir
set décor *m.*
set, to mettre
setting décor *m.*
seven sept
seventeen dix-sept
seventy soixante-dix

several plusieurs
sew, to coudre
sewing couture *f.*
shadow ombre *f.*
shake, to secouer
share part *f.*
shave, to raser
shaving brush blaireau *m.*
shaving cream crème à
   barbe *f.*
shaving soap savon à barbe *m.*
she elle
sheep mouton *m.*
sheet drap *m.*
sheet of paper feuille de
   papier *f.*
shell, egg coque *f.*
shellfish soup bisque *f.*
shine, to (shoes) cirer
ship bateau, navire *m.*
shipment livraison *f.*
shirt chemise *f.*
shoe soulier *m.*, chaussure *f.*
shoemaker cordonnier *m.*
shop boutique *f.*
shop boutique *f.*, magasin *m.*
   faire des courses
short court,-e
shorts caleçon *m.* (underwear)
short, in en somme
shoulder épaule *f.*
shout, to crier
show spectacle *m.*
show, to montrer
shower douche *f.*
shut, to fermer
shut up enfermer
sick malade
sickness maladie *f.*
side côté *m.*
sidewalk trottoir *m.*
sidewalk café terrasse *f.*
sign signe, pancarte, écriteau
   m.
sign, to signer
silent silencieux,-euse
silk soie *f.*
silverware argenterie *f.*
similar pareil,-le
simplicity simplicité *f.*
simply simplement

since depuis
   (because) puisque
sincere sincère, franc,-che
sincerely sincèrement
sing chanter
sir monsieur *m.*
sister soeur *f.*
sit down s'asseoir
six six
sixteen seize
size grandeur *f.*
   (clothing) taille
   numero . . .
skate, to patiner
skating patinage *m.*
skating rink patinoire *f.*
ski ski *m.*
ski, to faire du ski
skid, to déraper
skin peau *f.*
skirt jupe *f.*
sky ciel *m.*
skyscraper gratte-ciel *m.*
slander médisance *f.*
sleep, to dormir
sleep, go to s'endormir
sleeping-car wagon-lit *m.*
sleeve manche *f.*
slice tranche *f.*
slip, to glisser
slip combinaison *f.*
slipper pantoufle *f.*
slope pente *f.*
slowly lentement
small petit,-e
smell, to sentir
smile sourire *m.*
smoke fumée *f.*
smoking compartment
   fumeur *m.*
snapshot instantané *m.*
snow neige *f.*
snow, to neiger
soaked trempé,-e
soap savon *m.*
sock chaussette *f.*
soda water eau gazeuse *f.*
sofa canapé *m.*
soft mou, molle
soldier soldat *m.*
sole semelle *f.*

some des, quelque, quelques-
uns
sometimes parfois,
quelquefois
somewhere quelque part
so much tant, tellement
son fils m.
song chanson f.
soon bientôt
sore throat mal à la gorge m.
sorrow peine, douleur f.
sorry désolé,-e
soul âme f.
sound, to sonner
soup potage m.
south sud m.
Spanish espagnol,-e
speak parler
special delivery letter express,
pneumatique m. (in Paris)
specify préciser
spectator spectateur m.
speed vitesse f.
spend, to dépenser
spite of, in malgré
splendid splendide
split, to fendre
spoil, to gâter
sport sport m.
sporting sportif,-ive
spot endroit m.
spread répandre
spring ressort m.
spring (season) printemps m.
spirits of ammonia
ammoniaque
sponge éponge f.
spoon cuillère f.
sport coat veston m.
spring printemps m.
square carré,-e
square place f.
stage scène f.
stained glass window vitrail m.
stairway escalier m.
stamp timbre m.
standing debout
star étoile f.
starch amidon m.
starch, to empeser
start, to commencer

state état m.
statement déclaration f.
stationery store papeterie f.
stature taille f.
stay séjour m.
stay, to rester
steal voler
steam vapeur f.
steering wheel volant m.
stick bâton m.
still encore
stocking bas m.
stomach estomac m.
stomach ache mal au
ventre m.
stop, to arrêter
stop arrêt m.
stopover escale f.
store magasin m.
storm tempête f., orage m.
story (floor) étage m.
strange curieux, étrange
strawberry fraise f.
street rue f.
strike grève f.
string ficelle f.
strong fort,-e
student étudiant,-e
study, to étudier
study étude f.
subject propos, sujet m.
subordinate, to subordonner
subscribe s'abonner
subsidize, to subventionner
subtle difference nuance f.
suburb banlieue f.
subway métro m.
succeed réussir
such a tel,-le
sudden soudain,-e
suddenly tout à coup
suffer souffrir
suffice suffire
suffocate étouffer
sugar sucre m.
sugar-bowl sucrier m.
suit complet, costume m.
suit (woman's) costume
tailleur m.
suitcase valise f.
sum somme f.

summer session cours de
    vacances *f. pl.*
summer été *m.*
sumptuous somptueux,-euse
sun soleil *m.*
sun bath bain de soleil *m.*
sun-burn coup de soleil *m.*
sun glasses lunettes de soleil *f.*
Sunday dimanche *m.*
sunrise lever du soleil *m.*
sunset coucher de soleil *m.*
superb superbe
superior supérieur,-e
supervise surveiller
supper souper *m.*
supply, to munir
support soutien *m.*
supposed to censé,-e
sure sûr,-e
surely assurément
surprise surprise *f.*
surprise, to surprendre
surround entourer
suspect, to se douter de
suspenders bretelles *f.*
sweet sucré,-e, doux, douce
swell épatant,-e
swim, to nager
swimming nage *f.*
Switzerland Suisse *f.*
sympathy sympathie *f.*
symptom symptôme *m.*
syndicate syndicat *m.*
synonym synonyme *m.*
system système *m.*

T

table table *f.*
tablecloth nappe *f.*
tailor tailleur
take prendre
take advantage of, to profiter
take along emener
take care of s'occuper de
take off, to (aviation) décoller
talent talent *m.*
taste goût *m.*
taste, to goûter
tax impôt *m.* taxe *f.*
taxi taxi *m.*

tea thé *m.*
teach, to enseigner
teacher professeur *m.*
technique technique *f.*
telegram dépêche *f.*
telephone, to téléphoner
telephone téléphone *m.*
telephone book annuaire *m.*
    bottin *m.*
telephone booth cabine
    téléphonique *f.*
telephone call coup de
    téléphone *m.*
telepone operator
    téléphoniste *m., f.*
tempest tempête *f.*
tempt tenter
ten dix
tendency tendance *f.*
tender tendre
tennis tennis *m.*
term terme *m.*
terminal terminus *m.*
terrace terrasse *f.*
terribly terriblement
thank, to remercier
thanks merci
that ça, cela, ce, cette
the le, la, les
theater théâtre *m.*
theirs le leur
them eux, elles
then puis
there là
there is, are voilà
therefore donc
thermometer thermomètre *m.*
these ces, ceux
they ils, elles
thing chose *f.*
think penser, croire, réfléchir
third troisième
third tiers *m.*
thirst soif *f.*
thirteen treize
thirty trente
thirty-seven trente-sept
this ça, celui, celle, ceci, ce, cet,
    cette
thought pensée *f.*
thousand mille

thread fil *m.*
three trois
throat gorge *f.*
throw, to lancer
thunder tonnerre *m.*
Thursday jeudi *m.*
thus ainsi
ticket collector contrôleur *m.*
ticket office guichet *m.*
ticket window guichet *m.*
tight étroit,-e, serré,-e
time temps *m.*, fois *f.*
time table horaire *m.*
tip pourboire *m.*
tire pneu *m.*
tire, to fatiguer
tired fatigué,-e
to à
toast toast *m.*
tobacco tabac *m.*
tobacco store bureau de
    tabac *m.*
today aujourd'hui
together ensemble
toilet toilette *f.*, cabinet *m.*
tomato tomate *f.*
tomb tombeau *m.*
tomorrow demain
tongue langue *f.*
too aussi
too much trop
tooth dent *f.*
toothache mal aux dents *m.*
toothbrush brosse à dents *f.*
tooth paste pâte dentifrice *f.*
toothpick cure-dent *m.*
top haut *m.*
torture, to torturer
touch, to toucher
tough dur,-e
tour tour *m.*
tournament tournoi *m.*
toward vers, envers
towel serviette *f.*
tower tour *f.*
town ville *f.*
town hall mairie *f.*
toy jouet *m.*
track voie *f.*
traffic circulation *f.*
traffic jam embouteillage *m.*

tragedy tragédie *f.*
train train *m.*
trait trait *m.*
transaction transaction *f.*
transatlantic transatlantique
travel, to voyager
traveler voyageur,-euse
travelers check travelers
    chèque, chèque de
    tourisme *m.*
tray plateau *m.*
treat, to traiter
tree arbre *m.*
trimming garniture *f.*
trip voyage *m.*
trolley tramway *m.*
trouble peine *f.*
trousers pantalon *m.*
truck camion *m.*
true vrai,-e
trunk malle *f.*
truth vérité *f.*
try, to tâcher, essayer
Tuesday mardi *m.*
turn, to tourner
turret tourelle *f.*
tuxedo smoking *m.*
twelve douze
twenty vingt
twenty, about vingtaine *f.*
twice deux fois
twin beds lits jumeaux *m.*
two deux
type sorte *f.*, genre *m.*
typewriter machine à écrire *f.*

U

ugly laid,-e
umbrella parapluie *m.*
unaware of, to be ignorer
uncle oncle *m.*
under dessous, sous
understand comprendre
underwear linge de corps *m.*
undo, to défaire
undress, to se déshabiller
unforeseen imprévu,-e
unfortunate malheureux,-euse
unfortunately
    malheureusement

unhealthy malsain,-e
uniformity uniformité f.
union, workers' syndicat m.
United States Etats-Unis m.pl.
university université f.
unknown inconnu,-e
unpacking déballage m.
unpleasant désagréable
until jusqu'à
up there là haut
upset contrarié,-e
upstairs en haut
urgency urgence f.
urgent urgent,-e
us nous
usages us m. pl.
use (custom) usage m.
use, to se servir de
useful utile
useless inutile
usher, to annoncer
utilize, to utiliser

V

vacancy vide m., lacune f.
vacant libre
vacation vacances f. pl.
vaguely vaguement
valley vallée f.
valuable précieux,-se
value, to estimer
veal veau m.
vegetable légume m.
vehicle véhicule m.
velvet velours m.
very très
vest gilet m.
vicinity environs m. pl.
view vue f.
vinegar vinaigre m.
visa visa m.
visit, to visiter
visit visite f.
visitor visiteur m.
vizor visière f.
voice voix f.

W

waist taille f.
wait attendre

waiter garçon m.
waiting room salle d'attente f.
wake up se reveiller
waken, to reveiller
walk, to marcher
walking marche f.
wall mur m.
wall clock pendule f.
want, to vouloir
war guerre f.
wardrobe armoire f.
warm chaud,-e
warm, to chauffer
warn, to prévenir
wash, to laver
wash basin (fixture) lavabo m.
wash basin cuvette f.
watch montre f.
watchmaker horloger m.
watch out gare à vous
water eau f.
wave onde f.
wave hair, to faire onduler
   (les cheveux)
we nous
weak faible
wear, to porter
weather temps m.
Wednesday mercredi m.
week semaine f.
weigh peser
well! tiens!
west ouest m.
wet mouillé,-e
what quoi, quel,-e
wheat blé m.
wheel roue f.
when quand
where où
whereas tandis que
which que, quel,-e
white blanc, blanche
who qui lequel, laquelle
whom qui
why pourquoi
wicket (gate) portillon m.
wide ample
wife femme f.
willingly volontiers
win, to gagner
window fenêtre f.

window display étalage
wine vin *m.*
wing aile *f.*
wish souhaiter, désirer
with avec
without sans
witness témoin *m.*
witty spirituel,-le
wolf loup *m.*
woman femme *m.*
wonder, to se demander
wonderful merveilleux,-euse
wood bois *m.*
wool laine *f.*
word mot *m.*, parole *f.*
work ouvrage *m.*, œuvre *f.*
work, to travailler (people)
    marcher (machines)
workshop atelier *m.*
world monde *m.*
worldly mondain,-e
worry souci *m.*
worse pire, pis
worth, to be valoir
worthy digne
wrap up, to envelopper
wrench clef *f.*
wrinkle, to froisser

wrist watch bracelet-
    montre *m.*
write écrire
writer écrivain *m.*
writing paper papier à
    lettres *m.*
written écrit,-e
wrong tort *m.*
wrong, to be avoir tort,
    se tromper

Y

year an *m.* année *f.*
yellow jaune
yes oui, si
yesterday hier
yet encore
you tu, vous
young jeune
your vos, votre
yours vôtre
youth jeunesse *f.*

Z

zero zéro *m.*
zipper fermeture éclair *f.*